IN PRAISE OF LAZINESS AND OTHER ESSAYS

IN PRAISE OF LAZINESS AND OTHER ESSAYS

Indrajit Hazra

SIMON & SCHUSTER

London · New York · Sydney · Toronto · New Delhi

YODAPRESS

First published in India by Simon & Schuster India and Yoda Press 2024

Simon & Schuster: Celebrating 100 Years of Publishing in 2024

1 3 5 7 9 10 8 6 4 2

Simon & Schuster India
818, Indraprakash Building,
21, Barakhamba Road,
New Delhi 110001.

www.simonandschuster.co.in

Yoda Press
79 Gulmohar Enclave
New Delhi 110049
www.yodapress.co.in

Paperback ISBN: 978-81-946430-5-0
eBook ISBN: 978-81-946430-8-1

Typeset in India by SŪRYA, New Delhi
Printed and bound in India by Replika Press Pvt. Ltd.

To my partner in crime, O.

CONTENTS

BY WAY OF INTRODUCTION

Irreverent, Irrelevant

At the very outset—it really is an onset though, as you will find out soon enough—this collection of essays has no theme, no spine running through it holding it together, no gurgling brook joining the start to the end, no agenda, no party plan. My day job at the papers keeps me tethered to that kind of rubbish. Here, I have just one purpose and pleasure: to tell you things. Baas.

The very fact that these essays are not connected to the hum and the hee-haw of constantly happening events, occasions, trends, interests, breaking news and joining dots, those things that go viral (or, in my late dear, as well as dear late uncle's words, 'go virus') and then go die by swift forgetting, make them immediately useless for information ragpickers and conversation junkies. They can pick up the latest book on all-encompassing thoughts on everything, or A Pillow-Biter's Guide to a Happy Life.

Considering what I intend to do during the passage of this book—tell you things—is wholly independent from what you expect essays as a writing species to do, both you and I have no expectations, barring one: pleasure. The title of this collection could well have been It's Been a Pleasure & Other Essays. But that would have been presumptuous of me even before you began.

It is no coincidence that 'leela' has pleasure and play knotted into one tight, light, tongue tip-tripping word that Nabokov would have instantly recognised. This *playsure* entails taking the light, slight and fanciful things seriously and imbuing the heavy, serious, hmmdrums with a state of lightness, even frivolity. Such is the talent of our age to churn boredom until it resembles lassi that we make information the end-all and be-all of all experiences, especially the reading experience. I have encountered people who do not read fiction because it 'serves them nothing real', while they find it perfectly reasonable to be unperturbed by 'fake news' or concocted information decked out as facts to serve as subtle agitprop. Between the walls of this book, you will find nothing useful—not for Spartacus, not for Kirk Douglas; not for bhakts, not for kambakhts.

So, if there is anything holding 'In Praise of Laziness, and...' together apart from spit and syntax, it should be dives, forays, digressions and digressions with detours in between, vortexes, cul-de-sacs, and hopefully burn marks from sliding too fast across one corner of a page to another corner of the next. If there is an image that can serve as a ballast, a seat-belt for the duration of this book, keep the Straightest of Faces in mind. Doesn't matter whose, doesn't matter what it looks like to you, this Straightest of Faces will keep our spacetime journey together. For, the hi-falutin and the lo-falutin are not mortal enemies but kissing cousins. Remember, life can be long and slow-falutin.

In these pages, I intend to perform the shamanic function of a middle-aged *old* monk—the kind who smiles benignly at people who parrot things like 'Oil is the next data,' 'Stay Hungry, Stay Curious,' and 'Age is just a number' while imagining hacking them to pieces that can be fitted in neat, hygienic zip-locked plastic bags. I shall share observations and machinations tied to popular, unpopular, high culture and (always) low politics, relooking at some over-looked, some over-cooked subjects in a 'carefully careless' way.

Subjects range from praising laziness in the way folly and idleness were once praised by certified intelligent people; a literary forensic report on the adult years of Sukumar Ray's 'Pagla' Dashu and Mark Twain's Huckleberry Finn; the tactical use of radical shyness to confine oneself to the indoors; to the erotic value of the electric blanket; an investigation into a people via an atypical Bengali phenomenon; the functions and features of public mournings, and the mysterious phenomenon of mishearing song lyrics. There's even a science fiction story bunged in because any meditationism on colonialism cannot be shared in isolationism from alien invasionism.

Two of the pieces here are undisguised and undisguisedly personal—one on my footballing loyalties, the other on my hate-hate relationship with kitchens. Writing both have finally cured me of whatever psychiatrists, psychologists and psephologists want people to worry about and come to them for.

Yes, the book you hold in your paws is irreverent. But at no point while reading it should the reader forget that its author would consider it worth *his* while if she or he finds reading these essays as pleasure-giving as irrelevant. With great power comes great pointlessness—and fingernails.

I.H.
Flight 6E 2413
Between Kolkata and Delhi
October 2023

IN PRAISE OF LAZINESS

for Probho

During my recent journey back from Kolkata to Delhi, not wishing to waste all the time I was obliged to be on Facebook, I preferred to spend some of it thinking over some topic connected with our common condition. And our common interest in our common condition.

But this, as you may have already conjectured, was a more challenging prospect to undertake than to just lob around one's brain like the tongue feeling the back of one's teeth as if to make a great oral survey that ends in nothing. It is, however, a comfort, and quite probably a luxury, for me to have you understand the importance that we attach to being lazy, and the equal salience I give to laziness for myself to actually make the effort to lift my laptop lid, resist the sirens of the Internet-connected world within this portable machine, discount nominally more serious unstarted as well as unfinished word documents, and offer my encomium to laziness.

To praise sloth, especially in the time we happen to live in, is to oppose a worldview that has overwhelming consensus and support, no matter what one's class, sexual, political, dietary or aesthetic predelictions and disinclinations may be. To do nothing is one thing, but to find merit in doing nothing is quite another. It is heresy. It is a pity that at least for the superstitious, who seek confirmation whether in the herd or in the paternal voice—this voice being gender-neutral—or in numbers they believe to be not deus but data, there is no temple or faith preaching the virtues of laziness. Such is the depth of the delusion that even the lazy, those adept at laziness, consider it a vice.

Industriousness has been an object of veneration throughout human life. One cannot speak for a dog sleeping in the summer shade, or a cat lazing in the winter sun, and whether for animals, idleness is indeed the apogee of successful existence in an otherwise hostile world. But from childhood, regardless of culture or civilisation, class or economy, we have been taught to the point of becoming hardwired that even as we have a tremendous capacity to be lazy, this capacity bears the same shame as our ancestors once held to the commission of sin.

I'm not sure why such a eulogy—and a defence of such a eulogy—almost always demands classical references to back it up. Perhaps it spares effort. Perhaps it makes one understand what was meant to be understood but somehow has not. But here, I do point to the almost always supine and dormant character from the Ramayan of Kumbhakarna, brother of Lanka king Ravan, and nomenklaturally one of my two uncles.

Much too much chatter, legitimate and scholarly included, inevitably occurs whenever the character of a classical text like the Ramayan or Mahabharat is tugged out of bed to give ballast to one's argument. 'How many Ramayanas? Three hundred? Three thousand? At the end of some Ramayanas, a question is sometimes asked: How many Ramayanas have there been? And there are stories that answer the question.' AK Ramanjun writes to open his famous essay, 'Three Hundred Ramayanas: Five Examples and Three Thoughts on Translation', for a University of Pittsburg conference in 1987.

You are more than familiar with this text bandied about by scholars to this day to counter notions of any ur-text nonsense in the collective imagination of the rabble. You will also then understand that for my purpose, the source of the Ramayan text from which I bring out Kumbhakarna as if out of a police van in downtown Thane matters not one jot, since in the description that follows, not only are the various sources similar or same, but that there is no public disputation on the matter. On Kumbhakarna, barring nuances that need not trouble either of us, there is agreement.

[On the other hand, while there are many Ramayans—effectively many Rams, certainly many Sitas and Ravans and Surpanakhas, a healthy batallion of Hanumans, and a tetrapack of Valmikis, including one turned-Bruce Waynereturned-to-Ratnakar-and-back-to-Valmiki again, little if anything has been oralised—or the other way round—about the many Ram Rajyas, by which of course, we mean the polis, the citizenry. Perhaps one variant, tucked away in some Minnesota library or as sonorous mutterings of a Ghazipur babaji, goes:

> Meanwhile, the people of Ayodhya were celebrating yet another wonderful year under the competent, kind and happy King Bharat. Little did they know that in exactly two months to the day, the king's brother, thought to have died in exile somewhere in the south, would return and reclaim his throne. This sadness was ultimately overcome by that particular generation of Ayodhyans installing the pretence of celebrating the return of Ram, while in truth what they celebrated was the rule of the good, great king, Bharat.
>
> But onward to the one Kumbhakarna.

Sleep being the most notable and visible brand ambassador of indolence, and Kumbhakarna being the most famous brand ambassador of sleep, he is laziness made flesh. I point you here to the sixtieth chapter of 'Juddho Kanda' (War Volume) in the prose transliteration from Sanskrit to Bengali of Valmiki's Ramayan.[1]

The Ramayan, being quite the didactic epic that many, including myself, have read without mandatory reverence, is a place where Kumbhakarna's habit of sleeping for nine years at a stretch is presented as an extreme form of narcolepsy by all transcribers of the epic—an illness that should invite opprobrium. In a way it is. In the Uttar Kanda right at the end of Valmiki's Ramayan—which, I remember you once telling a curmudgeonly scholar droning on about para-texts, is a classic example of a para-text entering the main text over time 'like 'Logan' in Marvel's 'Wolverine' franchise'—Kumbhakarna's 'curse' of novennial wakefulness is described as actually a boon sought by the demon prince from Brahma that goes terribly wrong. (In Arshia Sattar's abridged English translation of the Critical Edition of the Sanskrit text, *Valmiki Ramayana*, prepared by the Oriental Institute at MS University, Baroda, he is also described as the chap who 'sleeps under Brahma's curse'.)

Acting on the instructions of the king of the gods, Indra, who you are quite aware has always been the model for spinelessness for me, Saraswati, the deity of Logos, entered Kumbhakarna and tricked him into seeking 'nidravatvam' (sleep), instead of 'nirdevatam' (the annihilation of the gods).

What I tend to find interesting is that despite this explanation that clearly puts the desire to do nothing (but sleep) in the 'curse' category, earlier, in the Juddho Kanda, when Ravan gives the order to wake his brother prematurely because of enemies at the gate, the reader doesn't find Kumbhakarna in such a bad state that curses usually imply. His abode is descibed as being voluminous because of the resident's size. But it is also filled with savouries and the sweet smell of flowers. After much cajoling, and then downright making a massive racket that includes some thousand elephants trampling along the giant demon's supine body, he finally wakes up.

The consequences of a sudden spike in metabolism—from an interruption of years of sleep—is hunger and thirst. Kumbhakarna is then described to consume buffaloes, pigs and all kinds of meat washed down by gallons of blood, fat and alcohol. It is only after he gets acclimatised from the world of inaction to the world egging him on to act that he politely asks in a 'sweet voice': 'What's happened? Why did you massage me so lovingly to wake me up? Is everything alright with King Ravan?' He is our empowered, entitled Gulliver.

In essence, Kumbhakarna is what the philosophers and other lifestyle commentators would describe as an Epicurean, a pleasure-seeker, a sensualist. The paradox here, of course, being that the chaser of sensory experiences finds it in sleep, the (partial) shutdown of all the senses. One can actually see what one is up against when one looks at a visual representation of the episode of people trying to wake Kumbhakarna. Even by 17th-century feudal Rajasthani standards, this painting by studio master Sahib Din from the illustrated Ramayan commissioned by Rana Jagath Singh of Mewar, shows much labour being put into things by everyone, except for the supine giant spreading across the picture.[2]

Slumber is underrated: *'The Awakening of Kumbhakarna,' Mewar Ramayan, Book 6, 'Yuddhakanda', c. 1650, Sahib Din, British Library*

One may find something comic in what the smaller figures are doing—prodding, poking, jabbing, pounding with tridents and maces. One Boschean pair next to Kumbhakarna's head seem to be in a heated exchange, in all probability dismissing the other one's tactic of waking the demon up and insisting that his own methodology is better. Even the quartet of musicians on the left are making an effort, via tune, via amplitude and certainly by avoiding anything too sonorous, soothing or soporific from the two stringed instrumentalists among them. You can almost taste the leathery salt sweat built up on the elephants in the background as their mahouts prod their ankushes deeper into the poor animals' soft heads to have them trample and pound on the reposing body with more gusto. All that effort to convert inertia into action must be tiring.

However, I am here not to bury labour, but to praise laziness. Milan Kundera, that fine writer whom we both have had only good, praiseworthy things to say about, faults the world we have come to inherit for our current antipathy against happy idleness. And he places this blame squarely, in his slim 1995 novel, *La Lenteur* (Slowness), on the modern, post-industrial cult of speed:

> Why has the pleasure of slowness disappeared? Ah, where have they gone, the amblers of yesteryear? Where have they gone, those loafing heroes of folk song, those vagabonds who roam from one mill to another and bed down under the stars? Have they vanished along with footpaths, with grasslands and clearings, with nature? There is a Czech proverb that describes their easy indolence by a metaphor: 'They are gazing at God's windows.' A person gazing at God's windows is not bored; he is happy. In our world, indolence has turned into having nothing to do, which is a completely different thing: a person with nothing to do is frustrated, bored, is constantly searching for the activity he lacks.[3]

I would venture to guess that upon reaching the word 'bored' in the Kundera passage I have quoted, you let out an indulgent smile. Perhaps my frequent diatribes against boredom have led you to believe that I may have, at the haunting midday of my life, finally come to terms with boredom, and perhaps even be holding out an olive branch or a conciliatory drink to settle down with an old antagonist Moriarty-Holmes-style, simply because I am now holding a brief for laziness, or because I am held hostage to the lazing age. Quite the contrary. Boredom, as Kundera points out, is the craving to engage. Laziness is the attainment of the desired condition of disengagement. It is saying, 'Enough of engaging' not with a sigh, but with the final positioning of many final positionings of pillows—both under head and between the legs.

Our nature is, I suppose for perfectly existential and evolutionary reasons, inclined in favour of action. After all, human greatness has been defined by it, while the opposite has been defined not in failure to take up a course of action—although Neville Chamberlain's attempt to 'appease' Hitler has been projected, in hindsight, as a desire not to act—but to either take up a course of action and fail, or to lead it to conequences that have proved unfortunate for men. Greatness becomes enjoined with action. At best, pussilinamity has been seen as inaction's muse.

But like the number of unborn outnumbering both the living and the dead, there have been enough angels who consciously decide, *without fear*, not to tread where many fools have sought to rush in Mel Gibson-as-William Wallace style. Laziness is not the first refuge of the scoundrel. It seeks to take leave from both justice and injustice alike. It chooses to leave the field altogether. Whether it can in this sublunary world is another matter. But not seeking something because it cannot be found in its full roundness is cowardice, an active force too many times conflated with indolence.

And it is this brave, underrated and unappreciated aspect of laziness that I present in your diwan-i-khas. Hopefully, I won't make out indolence to be just a simplistic decision to *not do something*, but as a force to *do nothing*, especially when the alternatives—both doing nothing and not doing something—are to risk facing as well as doling out pain.

The great writer Shibram Chakraborty not only understood the value of laziness but had the genius to distinguish being lazy from being idle. For him, indolence is a force that through the green fuse drives the flower, the kinetic charmed into potential, the wind humbled into air. In a 1972 interview conducted by Amitabh Basu in his column 'Dainandin Jibone' (In Everyday Life) where in every issue of the film magazine, *Ultoroth*, Basu posed a set list of questions to writers, Shibram had articulated the *nous* of laziness.

Replying to the very first question, 'When do you get up in the morning?' he sets the warp, woof and tone:

> It depends on the time. I try to get up as soon as I wake up. But after sleeping all night I feel so tired that to clear that very tiredness I need to sleep a bit more. As I keep doing this, when it becomes impossible not to get up, when it looks bad, then I just have to get up from bed.[4]

This is languor as joie de vivre, the purest manifestation of freedom, life as unmovedness—until internal compulsion compels.

As a questioner, Basu is taken aback, and asks Shibram the obvious question, 'During the whole day when do you write?' The response is disarming:

> I don't feel like writing at all—whether at night or during the day. It's just that if I don't write, I won't get food on the table. So, for the sake of staying alive (without being under the influence of any muse) I write because I have to write. Like if a rickshawala doesn't pull the rickshaw he won't be able to eat, my situation is a bit like that...

And then the coup de grâce: 'I write the next day, because I know only too well that writing the next day won't last.'

This is not some social, Marxist exposition of the need for equitable labour, where the term 'working class' contains a perverted pride in working and an inverted shame for 'working for the man'. Your copy of Bertrand Russell's *In Praise of Idleness and Other Essays* is buried somewhere here with me. But I'd be damned if I hunted for it to shoot it down. But I did look up the title essay for the purpose of our current investigation, and the philosopher's argument of equating the need for people to unburden themselves of work with idleness—doing nothing or making 'spare time' (sic)—remains as myopic as his role in Mohan Kumar's atrocious, untrustworthy 1967 anti-war movie, *Aman*.

In the scene, Russell meets the cretinous Rajendra Kumar—*not* Manoj Kumar, as I keep thinking—who plays the role of Dr Gautamdas, a medical officer off to serve victims of the atomic bomb blasts in Hiroshima and Nagasaki. Russell plays Master Yoda to Rajendra's young padawan, giving him a spiel on pacificism (the voiceover translator introduces him as 'Lord Russell, shanti ke neta': 'I have the greatest admiration and approval for your project.

I hope with all my heart that you will be *sexsexful* in finding the cure.'

But I digress. For a man who well knew that the cessation of war is only one kind of peace and not peace itself, his praise of muscular idleness is both strenuous and misleading.

'I think there is far too much work done in the world. That immense harm is caused by the work is virtuous,'[5] Russell writes in his essay, and in this we are in agreement. He invites 'leaders of the YMCA to start a campaign to induce, good, young men to do nothing,' rightly adding that 'the morality of work is the morality of slaves, and the modern world has no need of slavery. But then he Das Kapitalutes and goes all poltico-socialite, suggesting working hours be reduced to four, and that people working to provide themselves 'necessities and elementary comforts of life', spending the rest of their time 'to use as [they] might see fit'. Ah, the Russellian wobble that sees matters only via negativa in terms of a leisure class whose dependence sits on the Herculean, perpetual labours of others. This is praising wakefulness for its ability to recall dreaming.

Leisure, in its modern Bertrand Ghat usage, is not our supreme act of the laze, or araam, which signifies both pleasure and stillness, and certainly not pleasure and activity-that-is-not-work. The industry built around leisure—the oxymoronic 'leisure industry' giving the game away—is frenetic, frantic, hectic, repugnant work, a pig with lipstick but a pig nonetheless. This, my friend, is where laziness remains a challenge as well as the holy grail, a guilty pleasure, not a workshop activity 'to destress' or some satsang gathering where the herd both gets off and gets it off. Most importantly, like sleep and death, laziness is an anti-social activity that should be valued for being against deterministic schemes and for rescuing the individual from the herd.

Being lazy is an act of defiance that allows nothing to happen in one's most immediate body politic. But here again, like in almost all walks and languid positions in life, some people are intrinsically more reclined, and inclined towards it than others. That laziness is an effect of happiness—and yet can be a cause for unhappiness in almost all cultures—can be explained not by some dopey, new age, half-levitating gibberish peddled by suave, sweet-Anglophoney bearded unsadgurus as well as lifestyle fifth columnists, but solely by the mechanics of dopamine production inside our heads.

Depending on the occasion and the site of one's brain, dopamine—or 3,4-*d*ihydr*o*xyphenethyl*amine*, as I call my favourite neurotransmitter when among friends—is released. This when and where determines a person's proclivity towards being lazy—or, as deviant lotophagoi with a Protestant work ethic would prefer—towards being industrious.

In the 2012 paper, 'Dopaminergic Mechanisms of Individual Differences in Human Effort-Based Decision-Making,'[6] published in *The Journal of Neuroscience*, researchers shared their findings of an experiment in which they had mapped the brain activities of 25 healthy subjects. It revealed that people who are willing to work more for higher rewards—the 'go-getters'—had higher release of dopamine in the left striatum and ventromedial prefrontal cortex, especially when 'probability of reward receipt was low'—that is, when the prize was tougher to get. In the case of slackers, the higher the release of, pardon the demotic dip, the 'happy hormone' in the bilateral insula region of the brain, the less their willingness to expend energy to win rewards.

So, as you and I suspected instinctively in the early 1990s, when staring at the blurry stars under the open sky on the basketball court of our university, and lying on our backs overwhelmed any desire to swat the mosquitoes that would drain us of blood and action, some are happy doing nothing, while some make it their lives' pursuit to pursue rewards. And it is laziness that ultimately protects, as much as nature allows protection, from the violence of nature and man.

Laziness avoids Sisyphus' idiocy, where the illusion peddled is that of the absence of agency. Instead, indolence celebrates the Ziziphus, or more precisely the fruit of the Ziziphus lotus tree, whose consumption got a bad press from Homer, as always blind to cultures that went beyond the Peloponnese.

Emanating from a person who walked away from 'it all' (sic), the Buddhist notion of *kausidya—le lo* in Tibetan—fares no better than the Greco-Christian terror of sloth. But it attempts to handle this fear of laziness by confusing what it really is, in its characteristic, foggy 'within is without, without is within' way.

Bruce Alan Wallace—founder of the Santa Barbara Institute of Consciousness Studies (sic),—pegs laziness down with the usual fairground precision:

> If a person is working sixteen hours a day, hellbent on earning a whole lot of money with absolutely no concern for virtue, from a Buddhist perspective you could say that is subject to *le lo*. A workaholic is clearly not lazy, but such a person is seen as *le lo* in the sense of being completely lethargic and slothful with regard to the cultivation of virtue and purification of the mind.[7]

It is best to sidestep this kind of hoodwinking, where not only have the goalposts been changed to drone on about something called 'spiritual sloth,' but the sport itself being played has been changed. This supposed Tibetan-Buddhist-Santa Barbara understanding of laziness is as misleading, at least for our investigation, as talk of football of the Tampa Bay Buccaneers is for a Mohun Bagan AC fan, even as new interest has developed in Internacional de Futbol Miami a.k.a. Inter Miami for the latter.

So, let's not go all Wendy and Karen, and refrain from getting waylaid by Circes. If there has been success in giving laziness its due importance, it won't be found in the cabal, Marxist-Russellian or mass narcotic. We get a snatch of it in Mark Twain, when he grabs the longhorns of laziness and has slacker de royale Huck Finn tell us about lonesomeness:

> ...I set down in a chair by the window and tried to think of something cheerful, but it wasn't of use. I felt so lonesome I most wished I was dead. The stars were shining, and the leaves rustled in the woods ever so mournful; and I heard an owl, away off, who-whooing about somebody that was dead, and a whippowill and a dog crying about somebody that was going to die; and the wind was trying to whisper something to me, and I couldn't make out what it was, and so it made the cold shivers run over me...[8]

It may seem that what Huckleberry is feeling is *ennui*—that lack of spirit, disaffection and listlessness that washes over young adults, among others so inclined, discovering old poetry or Dylan songs to feel like grown-ups. But if you register what he senses—stars, leaves, owl, nightjar, dog, wind—as opposed to what he says he feels, Huck is feeling the beauty of the laze.

The successful appropriation of the thought-word 'lazy', derived from the Proto-Indo-European 'las-' meaning 'weak' and subsequently Low Middle German 'lasich' conflating 'weak' and 'lazy', can be found in the wonderful Bengali word, 'lyad'. Scholars, in keeping with the spirit of the scholarship of the word, are unsure whether lyad is derived from the British English 'lethargy'—from the medieval Latin litargia (state of prolonged inactivity), which in turn came from the Greek lethargos—etymologically, lethe (forgetfulness) + argos (idle) inactive through forgetfulness—or the more straightforward American English 'laid-back'.

I would plump for the latter since there is no reason

why 1950s patois should provide less worthy pedigree than European ancestry even for the post-coloni-anal lot, especially since the latter originates from the relaxed posture of lying-sitting in a tilted-back chair. The easy chair, or the planter's chair, may have been a British colonial import, but this chaise longue with its two long arms extendable to keep the feet up, up and apart in the style of gynaecological examination chairs (minus the fiddling) remains a collective Bengali memory, not a Victorian one.

Ergo, lyad—whether languid, laid-back, or lethargic—becomes a celebration, stripped of Greek, Protestant notions of 'weakness'. In its consumption—'lyad khawa' literally meaning to consume laziness (and, in turn, be consumed by it)—is to enjoy such a wealth. The world at large has, in defiant snatches, shown late appreciation of laziness in popular culture. More than the cult appeal of the Coen Brothers' *The Big Lebowski* (1998), in which the Ulyssean hero is the arch slacker, Jeff 'The Dude' Lebowski played by Jeff Bridges, it is in the character of Floyd (surname unknown), played by Brad Pitt in the Tony Scott-directed *True Romance* (1993), that the West truly holds up the lyadkhor (lyad-eater) as a role model for the first time.

Floyd the anti-odalisque: *Brad Pitt in Tony Scott's True Romance (1993)*

Unlike The Dude, Floyd does not engage in in-between activities like bowling or unscheduled sex. He holds his own as a roommate, largely sprawled on the coach, cooled by a table fan and sustained by junk food, photons on a TV screen and marijuana—an item that seems to be the western equivalent of the bolster metonym for indolence, but this time stripped of its Orientalismanic 'Chinamen in opium dens' pose—barely moving, except in an underwaterly fashion. As others swirl around him in the freneticism that young people and members of the underworld are cursed with, Scott's ever-reclining Floyd is the true and masterful retaliation to the tradition of odalisques by the likes of Ingres, Renoir and Matisse dripping of Morococo clichés. Here is the Reclining Floyd in perpetual state of pre-parinirvana.

But I see you are already twitching your mouth, ready to interject, *screech in*, as they say, when the valiant enters a scene where a crime is about to be committed rather than a crime scene. It is not easy, I admit, to inculcate laziness, to master it so as to wring out pleasure from it instead of being pummeled by forces hostile to it. But who says that being lazy, to gaze upon the laze, is an effortless act?

Perhaps, tactical laziness is something that would better suit the mob within the mob who are either genuinely or jealously mortified by any praise of inaction. And perhaps, by providing the example of procrastination I can ruffle fewer feathers—admittedly a tiring act—and claim for indolence the prize that it justly deserves.

Procrastination is the kissing cousin of laziness. And, indeed, our family motto is 'Why do something today when you can do it tomorrow?' This may seem a horrendous tactic in the life finite, not to mention crowded in by an external world that one can hardly schedule never mind control. But here, I'd remind you of what we, as humans, are—not Russellian communal enterprises in search of the perfect equilibrium between work and play, but individuals like any cheetah, parakeet or manta ray.

While everyone was looking elsewhere, zoologist Charles Sutherland Elton observed, 'All cold-blooded animals spend an unexpectedly large proportion of their time doing nothing at all, or at any rate, nothing in particular.' Going by modern compilations of time budget data, including, Joan M. Herbers' 1981 study, 'Time Resources and Laziness in Animals,' mammals are largely inactive too. As Herbers states early on in her underrated study:

> Quiescence can serve some very important ecological functions. A motionless animal may be restricted in its movements because of digestive events, predator avoidance tactics, thermoregulatory necessity, or territorial advertising. However, functional and strategic considerations may not explain all circumstances of inactivity; rather, it is conceivable that, for many animals, a great deal of their quiescence has no ascribable ecological or physiological function, but represents 'laziness'. This term is unfortunately loaded with anthropomorphic connotations...Depending on parameters of food availability and metabolic demands...the process of searching for and acquiring food can occupy surprisingly small amounts of time, with the remainder perhaps devoted to inactivity. That is, the possibility of laziness is a direct consequence of an animal's foraging patterns.[9]

It is not my intention to equate foraging with all kinds of activities. After all, functional coitus in lions, usually lasting 12–15 seconds (and not lasting a minute in all animals, primates included) is hardly an appeal against decorative copulation among humans. The object of propagation of species has grown if not vestigial, in the case of humans, then at least ancillary—or, at any rate, should have, the same way religion can produce great music, but great music need not be inspired by religion.

So, instead of scuttering about in the attempt to

scutter about to fill up time with 'functional and strategic considerations,' the right thing to do as a *sentient* being is to grasp the value of doing nothing. Circumstances that have to do with reality will, in any case, prevent us from doing nothing all the time, death being a foregone conclusion. So lyad is to be praised, not to be buried. The harm that men do lives after them, the non-harmful through inaction is too oft interred with their bones.

Thus, the happier branches of knowledge are those which are more related to inaction, and by far the happiest men are those who have no traffic at all with any kind of external action and follow Nature, if not to stop effort, then at least to minimise effort, postpone effort, domesticate effort. And for that, first, my industrious friend, there is the need to lay down your arms, preceded by your back and proceeded by your legs.

Reclaiming the body is important. The virtues of a bolster—the paash balish, literally the 'side pillow' in Bengali—in inculcating proactive lyad was appreciated in the 3 September 1923 edition of *The Singapore Free Press and Mercantile Advertiser* by 'P.H.R.,' who describes how upon returning from the Straits after seven long years, and a few hours after checking into an 'up-to-date London hotel,' he had demanded of the startled chambermaid, 'Where is my Dutch wife?'

> I hope you moralists...will read further before you commit yourselves to approbium (sic) of a custom which is so firmly rooted. Absent-mindedly I have deprived you

> for the moment of the explanation of my seeming lapse from sanity in the presence of a chambermaid. Your approbium (sic) would be wasted...A Dutch wife is a wife only in name. I cannot conceive of the most persecuted of husbands treating his spouse with the brutality which is meted out to the harmless bolster which finds a place in every bed worthy the name to be slept on from Penang to Singapore, from Kota Raja to Deli.[10]

Buried in this faux admonishing of his readers, including a Singapore Free Press-reading chambermaid, in 1920s England, P.H.R., (perhaps unintentionally) uncovers a thread that your mentor, the Egyptian pianist, would name 'Orientalist' and associate with the European race propaganda project that saw—and sees—the East as sensual, corrupt, devious, *lazy*, tyrannical and backward. In the case of P.H.R. going temporarily and partially 'Native,' we have Malaysian social scientist Syed Hussein Alatas in his 1977 classic, *The Myth of the Lazy Native*, recall and unstitch the image of 'the indolent, dull, backward and treacherous [Southeast Asian] native' transforming into a 'dependant native requiring '[the West's] assistance to climb the ladder of progress'.[11]

Alatas goes on to quote the Derbyshire-born F.A. Swettenham, the first resident general of the Federated Malay States:

> Less than one month's fitful exertion in twelve, a fish basket in the river or in a swamp, an hour with a casting net in the evening, would supply a man with food. A little more

> than this and he would have something to sell. Probably that accounts for the Malay's inherent laziness; that and a climate which inclines the body to ease and rest, the mind to dreamy contemplation rather than to strenuous and persistent toil. It is, however, extremely probable that the Malay's disinclination to exert himself is also due to the fact that, in the course of many generations, many hundreds of years, he has learned that when he did set his mind and his body moving, and so acquired money or valuables, these possessions immediately attracted the attention of those who felt that they could make a better use of them than the owner.[12]

So, the need to not work is taken as a sure sign of racial laziness—from a self-described 'industrious' leisure class. Responding to another instance of selective sightings of indolence,' Atalas shrugs, with extreme irony and extremer justification:

> If the Malays preferred to be independent cultivators, did this make them indolent? Did not the Europeans in the colonies avoid manual labour? Did they not avoid coolie labour? Why were they not called indolent?

Ah, one man's indolence is another man's La Dolce Vita. But it is the bolster—ironic, that in its verb form is supportive and strengthening—wherein lies the metonym for sinful, deprecatory sloth. And in the wake of this disparaging light and its many refractions, laziness has suffered in reputation and praxis. I must, though, confess to have once fallen for Occidentalist traps and trappings myself, when checking into a not-too-up-to-date Kolkata hotel—The Pearl Hotel with its Saidian restaurant-bar, Pasha; the young hotel attendant took me up to my room and before leaving asked me, 'Would you like a paash balish?' Which in my overthinking brain, not unhelped by the décor, I briefly thought could mean something akin to what P.H.R.'s hotel chambermaid may have thought a Dutch wife to be. But that matter was settled when I gratefully, and I hope gracefully, turned down the offer to bolster my chances of unwinding with 'Malayan' apathy.

I can see you are now waiting for a peroration, but it's silly of you to suppose I can remember what I've said when I've been spouting such a hotchpotch of words. There's an old saying, 'I'm lazy. But it's the lazy who invented the wheel and the bicycle because they didn't like walking or carrying things,' and here's a new one to put alongside it: 'Laziness could have stopped the world from hurting itself.'

And so I'll say goodbye. Lie back or lie down, lie and live well, daydream and nightdream, and stay free to choose and employ your human agency, distinguished initiates of LAZINESS.

Intermission

1 *Godye Balmiki Ramayan*, ed. Jyotibhushan Chaki, trans. Jyotibhushan Chaki, Ranendranath Bandyopadhyay, Kalyan Dasgupta, Bishyapati Chaki (2005, Deb Sahitya Kutir).

2 *Mewar Ramayana*, Book 6, 'Yuddhakanda', c. 1650, Sahib Din, MS 15297(1), f.64a, British Library.

3 *Slowness*, Milan Kundera, trans. from the French by Linda Asher, Rupa & Co, 1996.

4 'Dainandin Jibone', *Ultoroth*, Vol. 20 Issue 11, January 1972 Amitabh Basu.

5 *In Praise of Idleness and Other Essays*, Bertrand Russell, 1935 (Routledge, 1985).

6 'Dopaminergic Mechanisms of Individual Differences in Human Effort-Based Decision-Making,' Michael T. Treadway, Joshua W. Buckholtz et al., *The Journal of Neuroscience*, Vol. 32, Issue 18, May 2, 2012.

7 *Destructive Emotions: A Scientific Dialogue with the Dalai Lama*, Daniel Goleman, Bloomsbury, 2002.

8 *Adventures of Huckleberry Finn*, Mark Twain, Signet Classic, 1959 (1884).

9 'Time Resources and Laziness in Animals,' *Oecologia*, Vol. 29, May 1981, Joan M. Herbers, Department of Biological Sciences, Stanford University.

10 *The Singapore Free Press and Mercantile Advertiser*, September 3, 1923, https://eresources.nlb.gov.sg/newspapers/Digitised/Article/singfreepressb19230903-1.2.3

11 *The Myth of the Lazy Native: A Study of the Image of the Malays, Filipinos and Javanese From the 16th to the 20th Century and Its Function in the Ideology of Colonial Capitalism*, Frank Cass & Co, 1977 (Routledge, 2010).

12 *British Malaya*, Frank A Swettenham, Alan and Unwin, 1955.

A MAN OF THE GREAT INDOORS

I could have easily titled this essay 'an investigation into nationalism'. In fact, a certain variety of editor would have suggested—and I take suggestions as highly suggestive gestures—that I use the term 'nationalism' with high-camp irony, still an in-thing among literary-minded readers in English, I am told. But having a title on the lines of 'Investigating Nationalism' or 'Nationalism: A Study' or even the Romila Thapar-sturdy 'The Nous of Nationalism' would be me hoodwinking the reader, and hoodwinking them not on my terms. That would defeat the purpose of pleasure—the only purpose worth setting on the high table—rightaway.

But let me be honest. The nation, country, desh, ghar are all Dantean circles—some real, most not—that are successive compressions of The Outdoors. So, in a way, this *is* an investigation about nationalism, even nationhood, except that it takes the pillow cover and turns it inside out and will bring The Indoors to the centre-stage. The sense of *belonging* that The Indoors holds is nationalism, stripped of its vestigeal fat, shorn of the penumbras of its umbras. In effect, it's belonging to a space with deep romantic feelings without the outlandish bullshittery.

To wax eloquent about The Great Indoors, though, one must first examine what constitutes The Indoors. For which purpose, I must start by bringing The Outdoors, and our morbid fascination with it, a notch or two down. And here, there is no point starting with Westphalian or East Bengal notions of nationhood, but the romantic lyrical notions of Nature.

As an embodiment and brand ambassador of the exteriors, Nature has played a significant role in literature, in song, in cinema. The Outdoors comes 'readymade' (thus, the ease), and comes unmanhandled (thus, the charm). To taste The Outdoors one has to, perforce, step Outside, whether in a field of swaying kashphul (kasatandi in Odiya, kohuwa in Assamese, Sachharum spontaneum in Latin) rendered in unnatural black and white in Satyajit Ray's *Pather Panchali*, or by 'wandering as lonely as a cloud' to catch 'a crowd, a host, of golden daffodils' that too beside a lake, beneath fluttering and dancing trees. A large part of the modern vacation comprises a communion with (these avatars of) The Outdoors, with an ideal condition of living in such surroundings, perhaps the Kanchenjunga from your balcony or the Bay of Plenty from your office window. Yes, of course and ah!, this castafioric beauty can be past compare. But perhaps as a rupture to the natural cycle of daily life.

But The Outdoors is hardly about the bucolic plague alone. For an overwhelming number of humans, it means outside the confines of home and work but outside—*out* on the streets, eating *out*, going *out*, *out* for a walk, *out* shopping, *out* and about in town...Even in this Golden Age of The Indoors, where for functional purposes, food, entertainment, information and social encounters can be brought inside one's house, The Outdoors keeps up with its siren song and all able or moderately able-bodied landlubbing sailors comply.

A room or a balcony with a view is not universal. So, the charms of the city or town, and the exchanges made with other people as middlemen remain. It is this charmed circle of circles, when extended to a preposterous extreme (but not the extremest) that brings us to the notion of country, the domesticated, cow-bell sountracked term for nation.

Benedict Anderson's definition, as articulated in his 1983 book, *Imagined Communities: Reflections on the Origin and Spread of Nationalism*, still holds well, despite scrutiny from a new line of barbaric critics with leather elbow-patched jackets at its Resident Welfare Association gate:

> [The nation] is an imagined political community—and imagined as both inherently limited and sovereign. It is imagined because the members of even the smallest nation will never know most of their fellow-members, meet them, or even hear of them, yet in the minds of each lives the image of their communion.

The Outdoors facilitates this imagining, this notion of shared identities and experiences that one can cherrypick to retrofit one's sociophilic tendencies to belong. If the glue of language doesn't quite fit ('Why can't he speak in Hindi/English?'), then a buffet menu of culture has to do the trick ('Surely he follows IPL/Hindi movies/Classic Rock, or enjoys biryani/Diwali/Narendra Modi?). Anderson's largely fabricated community is augmented/virtual reality (AR/VR) at its most entrenched and prevalent. And when these shared identities and experiences don't quite happily coalesce into one giant saare jahaan se achha or über alles blob, instead of confronting the terribly rickety structure one apparently inhabits, one engages to mend the fissures. In other words, the spit and duct-taped entity is protected by sheer Schopenhauerian representative willy-nilly, while outliers and anomalies are made to bear the brunt of being a spanner in the works of a giant socialistic garden project that almost everyone wants to tend to.

Ironically, it is the rejection of this AR/VR that makes for a Man of the Great Indoors. (The Woman of the Great Indoors certainly predates this entity.) Ironic, because one would have thought that, at least, for those who can afford the infrastructure of WiFi, smartphone, digital payment, videophony, delivery apps, a pleasant view and enough (but not too much) BHK per sq. ft space, The Indoors would become the sanctum sanctorum, the venue of overwhelming existence, the city, the nation.

Did someone say social interaction? Followed by repeating that phrase this time prefixed with the word *real*?

Stepping out to meet people, and be met by them, is a necessary function of life. The irony of going away, *out* there, to get away from people is something I can chuckle-cum-snigger at alone later. But for now, let me try and dismantle the *social* need among post-hunter-gatherers to go *out*.

Passengers: *Iggy Pop in concert, Cincinnati, Tom Copi/Getty Credit: Wiki commons*

In 1992, anthropologist and evolutionary psychologist Robin Dunbar published a paper in the *Journal of Human Evolution* with the title, 'Neocortex size as a constraint on a group size in primates'. On paper, it doesn't sound much to do with contemporary human behaviour. But what Dunbar was suggesting was that the bigger an animal's brain—actually, the volume of the neocortex, or the outer layer of the neural tissue of the cerebrum in mammals—the higher their social and cognitive abilities.

> ...the number of neocortical neurons limits the organism's information-processing capacity and that this then limits

> the number of relationships that an individual can monitor simultaneously. When a group's size exceeds this limit, it becomes unstable and begins to fragment. This then places an upper limit on the size of groups which any given species can maintain as cohesive social units through time.

By 2003, Dunbar, along with fellow anthropologist Russell Hill, got down to a specific species—and a specific number—in the *Human Nature* paper, 'Social network size in humans'. Remember Mark Zuckerbhai is still a year away from F-wording his idea of a social network. The findings in Russell's and Dunbar's study were limited to 'social network size in contemporary Western society based on the exchange of Christmas cards'. In effect, a number of people were asked to make a list of all those to whom they sent Christmas cards. On an average, 68 cards were sent to households that totalled about 150 members.

What is interesting is not so much that Western and Eastern, Northern and Southern societies alike have since 2003 discovered the virtues of WhatsApp messages and forwards to scatter festive greetings pixie-data, but that 150 seems to be the consistent maximum number predicted for a human's social network size based on the size of the human neocortex. This is akin to pre-industrial societies where clans—usually groupings based on common ownership of a hunting area, etc.—according to census data have an average size of 153. Also true of businesses where a firm comprising less than 150 people work fine on a face-to-face basis, but need a formal hierarchy once they grow larger than 150 people to function well.

As Dunbar elaborates in his 2010 book *How Many Friends Does One Man Need?* that makes him sound like he always wanted to be a folk singer, 'What keeps the community together is a sense of mutual obligation and reciprocity, and that seems to break down once community size exceeds about 150.' And this is Dunbar's number: 150—'...the set of people who, if you saw them in the transit lounge during a 3 a.m. stopover at Hong Kong airport, you wouldn't feel embarrassed about going up to them and saying: "Hi! How are you? Haven't seen you in ages!"'

Of course, Dunbar's Number, the number of people with whom one can maintain stable social relationships itself comprises a flexible hierarchy set in consecutively larger circles: 5 loved ones, 15 good friends, 50 friends, 100 meaningful contacts, the rest being acquaintances, and finally those you can recognise.

Some folks tend to mix these categories up, with embarrassing consequences. I have a friend who lives abroad whom I met after ages at a restaurant. On entering the place he assured me, 'I know the owner well. Let me get us the best seats in the house.' He did his usual politer version of snapping one's fingers, dropping of name, asking how so-and-so is some 15 years after he had last met so-and-so. Polite but blank faces returned his request. To my mind, we got better seats in the house—next to the window overlooking the street—but my friend had clearly mistaken one Dunbar circle for another.

Believing in the nation beyond differentiating yours from another's is pretending Dunbar's Number doesn't exist. And even if one recognises its existence, then it's a fabrication that Dunbar Circles keep expanding to include utter strangers: both 'known strangers' you may catch a glimpse of on a bus or 'unknown strangers' whose existence you haven't registered because you cannot.

The closest model to the nation in this Benedictine sense is Facebook. I have 3,304 Facebook Friends. Simply, by dint of calling them 'friends', the Zuckerberg Club has collapsed all categories of people I am 'socially' in contact with into one single category, my friends. So, my father who is not on Facebook—that he has a phone is sometimes seen as a lapse of judgement on his part—makes him, in the Facebook metric, a stranger to me, at par with a lady in Venezuela who was a close friend and confidante of the artist Balthazar Armas, whom I also never knew until I just Google Searched 'Venezuela artist'.

So The Outdoors, at times beautiful, inviting, celebrated as being alive and planetary, is also ugly, hostile, but above all, unfamiliar, and therefore, quite genuinely 'unfriendly'. But even the unfamiliar Outdoors that thrills us with its unfamiliarity—new places, geographies that one discovers and finds amenable or even pleasurable, or even fills us with awe—does not serve the function that places one is fond of does: favouritism.

It would be ridiculous for the Indian patriot, for example, to extol the virtues of patriotism by stating how much he adores Egypt. According to the very rules of national pride, one is supposed to take pride in one's own nation, by one's familial. And by account of this definition of the beloved familial, nationalism falls woefully long, overextending itself to literally ridiculous lengths and breadths. How, pray, can you honestly treat a person in Bhatinda as falling in your circle of fondness—by dint of being only 'a fellow Indian'—when you can maintain genuine social feelings towards 150-odd people?

Hence, the invention of fellowship and affinity tools like a flag, a pledge, an anthem, a social media platform, a club membership, a sports team...a nation.

'Desh' and 'ghar', both as words and the things they represent, are far more dexterous—in today's unbearably stolid language, 'fluid'—in capturing what 'nation' desperately strives to attain and fails beyond the metaphysical. Because 'desh' contains the physical and the visible solidness of home, village (the city somehow, unfairly, never made the grade), the country in *country*side. Even 'ghar'—as in ghar wapsi, or homecoming—which I constantly confuse while speaking in Hindi to mean the Bengali 'room' contains not just the indoors of one's home, but its immediate surroundings, its neighbourhood. So when someone sends out the message, 'Har ghar tiranga', in my head, my neocortex to be precise, I also hear the directive, 'The tricolour in every country'.

My country is the familiar, the large familial. Fondness and loyalty comes automatically and develops like moss over time. I owe allegiance of sorts, love of the kind that's certain, hatred also of that sure kind, towards Mayur Vihar (all three phases) in east Delhi, and Kalitala in Garia in extreme south Kolkata (technically, it falls under South 24 Parganas). My territorial loyalties once included Beleghata in east Kolkata where I spent the bulk of my childhood and all of my early youth. So, belonging is also a function of time.

This fondness is what nationalism seeks to mimic and overwhelm by sheer mythological force and size. Is much of this Patriotism fuelled by nostalgia? Much of it, yes, but not all, unless one considers habit to be nostalgia mahogany-framed. The strangely hard green benches at the courtyard of Samachar Market in Mayur Vihar are shorn of their coldness when one understands how integral they have become to one's back and buttocks. Familiarity may breed contempt among persons. But the indoors, and by extension the 'indoored outdoors'—one's ilakas, grazing grounds, waterholes, *living* rooms—do not judge, or talk back.

Being master of one's castle may sound twee, even wrong when internationalism—a scaled-up and diluted version of nationalism's brotherhood of man—is the liberal credo. But the sanctity of private property, like Jerry's hole in the wall from where he steps out regularly to duel with Tom, is to be questioned at the risk of questioning the value of the individual in a sea of humanity.

The world is not a terrible place despite what you hear from your sources. It is, however, full of terrors. One prime reason for that is what my friend Molière very clearly and rightly mentions in his wonderfully modern 1666 play, *Le Misanthrope ou l'Atrabilaire amoureux* (The Misanthrope, or the Cantankerous Lover): Le monde par vos soins ne se changera pas. The world will not change for all your meddling. The Indoors, you can rearrange.

I SINGE THE BODY ELECTRIC

The orgasm, if and when it arrives, is still the gold standard for all human pleasures. To achieve it, the brain starts to shut down and ignore all anxieties, fears and joys, until during that short stretch of turbulence—usually longer for women (if it is genuinely experienced) than it is for men (fudging it will require a deus ex machina)—it is drained of all emotions. Until, of course, emotions start filling up again with Archimedean inevitability once the job at hand, or otherwise, is done.

Everyone's favourite experience is measured against this brief and total shutdown of emotions. Whether it is sipping an 18-year-old Oban single malt whisky in a perfect setting, or listening to Bismillah Khan's 1987 Paris recording of *Raag Guri Todi* with your feet up (with or without an 18-year-old Oban within one's reach), or driving a Ferrari F40 full-throttle at the crack of dawn up and down Marine Drive, or biting into a piping hot jalebi from your favourite childhood shop (I have none in particular)...

Diving into such pleasures is seeking to temporarily

obliterate one's emotional self by overloading it with emotions triggered by the senses.

I have never been much of a connoisseur of such life-affirming devices. Happy participant, yes. Expert, no. This isn't because of a lack of trying or some complex class-hostility towards luxury as some of my friends may suspect me of harbouring; although the cult of the single malt whisky continues to puzzle and bemuse me. On the contrary, I have always been a worshipper of the luxurious experience, in the sense of its original meaning derived from the Latin 'luxuriosus', or having the quality of excess.

Which is why for me the ultimate luxurious material experience is lying on an electric blanket and being semi-toasted to sleep. In the Delhi winter, of course.

I can see that the needle's just skated off the vinyl like a scampering crab at the mention of an electric blanket as my most LME, luxurious material experience. Of all the gin joints in all the towns in all the world, I hear you mutter, you choose to walk into this one? Is this what makes me go, to quote Meg Ryan in *When Harry Met Sally*: 'Oh, oh, oh, god, oh god, ah, oh god, oh...oh god, yes, yes, yes, yes, yes, *yes, yes, yes, yes*!'?

Am I setting up this celebration of my relationship with the humble electric blanket as a cute, contrarian argument against expensive luxuries that are plastered all over websites, which are forwarded to me by people who wish to educate me in the epicurean delights that made grey days gorgeous, like sirens in full-song? Not at all.

I certainly believe that an overwhelming number of human experiences that deserve to be swooned over cannot, and do not come cheap. Money is still the least silly way of objectively measuring the value of anything, objects and phenomena providing pleasure included. Much thought, talent, craft, effort, pride and love is put into the many things that people have had the good fortune and/or means to enjoy.

Even as I write this, I can still feel some of the old luxuries I have experienced...

...eating a Kobe beef steak at a wonderful London restaurant; spotting whales in choppy South African waters; managing to read a page or two under dazzling starlight at the Cloud End Forest Reserve above Mussoorie (the book was a paperback copy of John Toland's *Adolf Hitler*); grinning the night away without any apparent reason after popping an ecstasy pill with friends in Mumbai; wearing my heavy black Doc Martens boots that magically keep my feet on the ground and my head in the clouds at the same time; guzzling copious amounts of Jameson, my favourite Irish whiskey with an 'e' (Blender's Pride, not much of a luxury item, is my favourite whisky) alone with my favourite music bouncing about in my living room with no smoking restrictions; staring at a landscape that contains the Himalayas, the Karakorams *and* the Hindu Kush in one frame from a pass near Chilas in Pakistan as the skylight dims and I relieve myself against a rock face (Karakorams)...

...and lying down on my electric blanket-covered bed on Delhi winter nights.

Current writing and reading tastes dictate that experiences good, bad or banal, *especially* banal—are recounted and given value by describing them in hyper-detail and pegging them to a particular time and place. Emotions are ascribed to minor events, making them major in an inflatable Proust-doll way. Feelings, the plankton that floats in all purple prose oil-spilled writing and considered a delicacy in a particular variety of English-read'n'smack lips circle, are strung up 'like pearls'. I prefer strung-ups of the hanging kind in prose—language that is ropey, dead weighty, all over the place but gravitationally held together, giving off gallows humour that can be detected over the pressed handkerchief but not overpowering enough for the reader to leave the scene. The clot can thicken, as long as the sentences do not a jot.

But my most LME is neither a tent in a field to be pegged down among a sea of hyacinths, nor one of those 'Remember the first time?' anecdotes that can expand accordion-like into a Facebook post, or even a novel, one leading increasingly to the other these days.

I not only remember the tactile pleasure and slow-simmering joy of my body in contact with the heat of the blanket beneath me for hours every night, but I also look forward to it like a child looks forward to torrential rain. I value this seasonal luxury over the singularly freakish.

The electric blanket—a mattress in fact, considering it is tucked *under* the bedsheet—came into my life more than 15 years ago when it arrived as a house-warming (sic) present.

Being summer when it entered my life, it came folded inside an oversized transparent plastic bag with handles. It would take months before the blanket could actually show me that it was not just another household gadget—an article of home furnishing that served no real functional purpose at all—but a precious cross between a hot water bottle and a bedsheet. The first winter, it would show me that the electric blanket is to the experience of lying down in the cold what the MiG-29 is to that of flying supersonic.

That electric blanket was made in South Korea and it was not lying when it proclaimed that it is 'Good Night: Luxury Electric Blanket'. The rectangular 135 cm by 180 cm patch of deftly stitched thick cloth contained heavily insulated carbon fibre wires which you can't feel even if you were the hypersensitive 'You-need-therapy-princess' princess in Hans Christian Andersen's *The Princess and the Pea*. It never covered the whole expanse of the bed, but negotiating the geographical edges of the blanket was part of the experience. Feeling around with the toe or the thigh or the elbow or the outside of my arm, I would encounter no-fly zones where heat and cold from either side of the ridge shot dead any sinewy stretch of lukewarm. Navigating the rim of the mattress, where the skin gazed into the abyss and the abyss glanced back at it, became an acquired skill.

Once this bed of lava is switched on, the world is flat. Maximising the body's surface area to soak up the heat from below is a strategic art. Limbs straying outside the blanket's satrapi truly fall off the edge of the world into the icy hell 'below'.

But the nerve centre of this engineering-cum-design treasure invented by an American doctor named Sidney Russell in 1912 is a white box the size of a TV remote handset. This is the temperature regulator that goes from the initial on-off click to the soundless 1 to 7. I have never had to cross the 2 mark. It is I who was lord and master, master manipulator, holding Manichean control of this regulator of two-dimensional micro-climate every winter since 2006 by turning the orange-glowing knob that rests on my side of the bed. It is I who was in control of this comfort. The hum of the regulator was the hum of my pleasure outsourced.

If the function and price (it was Rs 4,000 in 2006) of my first electric blanket suggests banality and relative cheapness for the price to pay if I did not have it, then it stands to reason that lying on a humming electric blanket in winter being my favourite luxurious material experience exposes my banal taste and penchant for cheap thrills.

But it is sprawled on an electric blanket that I have, for about four months every year, transformed each night from a banal man with a brainful of anxieties, fears and joys into a dead chieftain set adrift on a burning boat into the sea like in those old Norse sea burials, one of which the 10th-century Arab traveller-writer Ahmad ibn Fadlan described thus: '...the relatives of the dead chieftain arrived with a burning torch and set the ship aflame. It is said that the fire facilitates the voyage to the realm of the dead.' But unfortunately, the account does not tell to which realm the deceased was to go.

Valhalla, Inshallah: *The Viking's Burial (Des Wikings Bestattung), 1892, Alexander Zick*

And it is here that I have an advantage over those old Vikings. On an electric blanket, which feeds and is fed on 110-220 volts of steady low fire, I know my destination: a realm where there are no emotions. And here, the little death lasts not for seconds, but for hours.

BECOMING ADULT

Mr Finn and Dashorothi-Babu

All old people have been young. But not all young people have been old.

There is something exceedingly odd about children not reaching adulthood. The only thing that can match this oddity would be a crime novel whose last few pages have been ripped out and we never get to know who committed the crime. The death of children is profoundly sad on two levels—one, the cessation of life itself; two, being nipped in the bud, with the run never being allowed to break into sweat.

But children die. In fact, many, many children die. And many die well after infanthood. In other words, they pass away even as their tales have begun to be told, in *medias res*, unlike babies that are really still drafts, proto-humans.

Take Rana. Never really picked up his surname. He was my first ever friend who died. He lived a few houses away from ours, and was considerably older than the rest of us. But when you're six or seven, twelve or fourteen is not just considerably older, it's twice your age, and you are keenly aware of this because of the sheer difference in size.

But Rana, unlike other older boys in our horseshoe lane, fitted in with us half-his-agers, half-his-sizers perfectly well for two reasons: one, because he was fun and found our company fun; two, because he was what we would call 'special' today, what we called 'slow' yesterday, and the day before, something that sounds meaner, even cruel, today, but meant exactly the same as 'special' some 45 years ago.

Rana walked funny, with a huge limp that was more Commedia dell'arte than Byronic. He talked funny too, with a stutter that seemed to end each time in a violent, slapstick fall. But his crookedness was glorious when we played football in the weekday afternoons and Sunday noons. It was glorious because it was hardcore and physical. Because he was bigger than us in size, he was formidable. Because he was Rana, he was also unpredictable. It was as if Immanuel Kant was an older friend of his, describing the boy-man rather perfectly when he had written '...out of the crooked timber of humanity, no straight thing was ever made'.

Then one day, erratically, unpredictably, there was a hubbub in our lane. Grown-ups had gathered in front of Rana's neat, white one-storeyed house with the only 'landing' in the neighbourhood. Us kids, realising that something was wrong—and wrongness has a weird way of making an ordinary day exciting—ventured forth to find out what it was. It was the vanishing of Rana.

It later transpired (strange sweaty word that) that Rana

had quarreled with his family the evening before and had set out at dawn to leave home forever. But unlike Kanchan running off to the big city of Kolkata in Shibram Chakraborty's 1937 novel *Bari Theke Paliye* (Run Away From Home) or Dick Whittington off to seek his fortune in London, Rana must have ventured off to the nearby Subhas Sarovar, a large park area ringing a large lake for morning- and evening-walkers, where I had been pram-pushed around by my mother less than a decade before. He must have because after much looking for him high and low, Rana's body was found by the police in Subhas Sarovar, literally *in* the sarovar, the same lake where I had learnt to swim.

Rana was, at best, fourteen. At worst, sixteen. He would have been in his late 50s-early 60s today were he alive. He could have, as many tend to do, died in his 30s, 40s. But he didn't manage to reach the great plains of early manhood. He stopped at the foothills with a fuzz just about growing on his upper lip and chin.

Perhaps, the sorrow (from the Old English 'sorg/sorh': care, anxiety, grief) would have been less remarkable if Rana had not disappeared forever-fourteen. Compared to, say, when I encountered the first death of a loved one in the family a few years later, my grandfather's, Rana's death was like a ghost story, which today has turned into a 'What if?' story that starts:

> *The sun was going down rapidly through the vein-like branches of the trees on the other side of the lake. You could see the top*

> *of the stadium, taking in the last of the autumn rays. But what you could see above everything else were the shadows settling as the whole scene was pecked and punctuated by furious bird song. People lingered, but the birds were returning to their nests. In that ascending son et diminishing lumière, sitting on one of the exceedingly hard but pleasant seats that felt metal but was wood, he could not help return to the thought that he always had when returning to this spot: 'What if Rana had lived to grow up to be a man of similar middle age?'*

Real people, even boys, stay dead once they die. But what if Rana had been a fictional boy, a figment Freud? A concocted teenager whose story ended with him as being forever remembered as a boy, playing crooked football like Garrincha? Forever a boy spouting expletives—and Rana had a temper—like those under the watch of the 19th-century neurologist Gilles de la Tourette?

Before Rana, there were two fictional boys. *After* Rana, I discovered both of them separately and hold them up even now in my 50s as my heroes, role models to be emulated in what they could have become as men, since neither Huckleberry Finn a.k.a. Huck nor Dashorothi (no surname mentioned) a.k.a. Dashu knew middle-age. Or more correctly, neither knows middle-age to this day and never will.

So, Huck first. Dashu then.

***

We meet Huckleberry Finn first in Mark Twain's 1876 novel *The Adventures of Tom Sawyer*:

> Shortly Tom came upon the juvenile pariah of the village, Huckleberry Finn, son of the town drunkard. Huckleberry was cordially hated and dreaded by all the mothers of the town, because he was idle and lawless and vulgar and bad—and because all their children admired him so, and delighted in his forbidden society, and wished they dared to be like him.

Twain goes on to provide what real life would have provided without even trying if Huckleberry was real—his physical form:

> Huckleberry was always dressed in the cast-off clothes of *full-grown men* [my emphasis], and they were in perennial bloom and fluttering with rags. His hat was a vast ruin with a wide crescent lopped out of its brim; his coat, when he wore one, hung nearly to his heels and had the rearward buttons far down the back; but one suspender supported his trousers; the seat of the trousers bagged low and contained nothing, the fringed legs dragged in the dirt when not rolled up.

Then, what real life never provides: a person's state of spirit a.k.a. spiritual state:

> Huckleberry came and went, at his own free will. He slept on doorsteps in fine weather and in empty hogsheads in wet; he did not have to go to school or to church, or call any being master or obey anybody; he could go fishing or swimming when and where he chose, and stay as long as it suited him; nobody forbade him to fight; he could sit up as late as he pleased; he was always the first boy that

> went barefoot in the spring and the last to resume leather in the fall; he never had to wash, nor put on clean clothes; he could swear wonderfully. In a word, everything that goes to make life precious that boy had. So thought every harassed, hampered, respectable boy in St. Petersburg.

Dashu, the Bengali boy, is around the same age as the boy 'from the Missouri side of the mighty Mississippi River'. We are introduced to him in Sukumar Ray's short story, 'Pagla Dashu' (Mad Dashu), first published in the 1916 edition of the children's magazine, *Sandesh*. Outside the freeze-frame of fiction, in which direction we need to venture for this Gedankenexperiment, Huck is 40 years Dashu's senior; actually, probably about 75 years older, since Twain writes in his preface to Tom Sawyer that the 'period of this story' is 'thirty or forty years ago'. But the 29-year-old Ray's narrator is also looking back some 17 years in time to his school days, making Huck's and Dashu's age difference roughly 60-odd years—a generational difference in less culturally globalised times.

But trapped in the amber of perpetual boyhood, they are both 12–13 till the end of time.

Pagla Dashu's eponymous story starts also with public judgement and description of his physical attributes:

> Among all the students in our school, there was not one who didn't know Pagla Dashu. Even the person who knew nobody else would recognise Pagla Dashu before anyone else. A new guard had arrived that time, a total village bumpkin. But the moment he heard Pagla Dashu's

> name, he immediately figured out who Pagla Dashu would be. Because the structure of his face, the way he talked, the way he walked gave clues that his brain was a bit 'addled'. His eyes were perceptibly round, his two ears unnecessarily big, his head bearing a sackful of unruly hair. Looking at his features made one think—
>
> On thin body, short stature rests a heavy head
>
> As if Jessore's koi fish has taken a human manifest.
>
> When he walks briskly or speaks impatiently, the way he throws about his arms and legs, somehow one is suddenly reminded of shrimps.

His state of spirit is described thus in the same story:

> We always made fun of Dashu—ribbing him about his brains and looks in not so nice ways. But we never saw him get irritated. At times, he would add colour to our words and tell us weird stories about himself. One day he said, 'Guys, whenever anyone is making aamshotto in our neighbourhood, they call me. You know why?' We asked, 'You eat a lot of mango leather, do you?' He said, 'Not really. When they put out aamshotto to dry, I show myself on that terrace a couple of times. That alone makes all the crows all over fly away.

Dashu's self-deprecatory nature is alarming and disarming at the same time.

These two boys, joined by the elixir of eternal boyhood, from different places and different times than mine—and a different time is, by itself, a different place—however, belong to two different worlds. Huckleberry is poor, living a life of ramshackle poverty in pre-Civil War American South. In fact, if it wasn't for his seeming unawareness of the fact, his life is brutal, punctuated and bracketed by the sudden appearances of his drunkard, sadistic father who constantly berates him for trying to be above his—Huck's father's—social class and be co-opted by the society that he despises and constantly attempts to 'save' his son from.

Which is ironic, because despite his dear friend Tom's attempts to 'sivilize' him, most obviously by making him attend school with him, Huck is truly against society.

Under the guardianship of the 'Widow Douglas', though, he gives society a shot.

> [She] took me for her son, and allowed she would sivilize me; but it was rough living in the house all the time, considering how dismal regular and decent the widow was in all her ways; and so when I couldn't stand it no longer, I lit out.

When the Widow Douglas's sister, Miss Watson tells Huck to be good—by not doing all the things he did wrong, like putting his feet 'up there', 'scrunch up', 'gap and stretch'—so that he doesn't one day end up in 'the bad place', he finds the destination quite attractive. This opinion is strengthened when she tells him that *she* 'was going to live so as to go to the good place'. Huck does not think much of this 'good place', where according to Miss Watson 'all a body would have to do there was to go around all day long with a harp and sing, forever and ever'. He is more of a '*toutes les saisons en enfer*' guy.

Dashu, on the other hand, is chaos within the order of society, which in Ray's stories *is* the school. He is eccentric, intelligent, and popular, akin to the school prankster being respected. He shakes off authority, and is shaken by his shirt collars by authority whenever he is caught doing something 'improper'. And he's almost constantly wearing a grin, before or after one of his pranks, or even in the distance while the effects of his machinations are underway. What also holds us about Dashu's character is that even as a boy, he cannot tolerate injustice, whether meted out against him when he is told by a poncy classmate that he has no time to explain to him the meaning of an English word, or when it is directed at others. In all the four Pagla Dashu stories, his pranks are his tools for 'crime-fighting'.

Huck has no such desires, except for freedom. Complete freedom that Eric Fromm would have identified as both freedom *from* restrictions, and freedom *to* do whatever one chose. Both boys are anti-authoritarian. But while Dashu wants to belong, Huck doesn't, even though at times he seems happy to.

Ray's Dashorothi exists across a few pages, confined to the classroom or school grounds. We know nothing about his social milieu beyond it. But by dint of being in school—and wanting to belong—we can situate him in late 18th-early 20th century middle-class Bengal. Unlike Huck or Hamlet, there is no looming father clouding and overwhelming his formative years. What marks him out is his individuality, striking in its opposition to contemporary depictions in fiction of a 'subodh balok' or a good boy.

Much may be gleaned from the illustrations that accompanied the visual descriptions of the boys. The 1874 first edition of *The Adventures of Tom Sawyer*, illustrated by True Williams, introduces us to Huck in a grungier, more Victorian chimney-sweeper mode holding famously his procured dead cat ('Say—what is dead cats good for, Huck?' 'Good for? Cure warts with.'). In fact, Williams' portrait of a smiling Huck looking into the distance, barefoot, straw hat on his head, holding the black cat by the tail as if by briefcase handle, reminds me of the 1872 sketch by Paul Verlaine of the 18-year-old Arthur Rimbaud.

But it is the illustrations by Edward Winsor Kemble of Huck in Twain's 1884 sequel to *Tom Sawyer, The Adventures of Huckleberry Finn (Tom Sawyer's Comrade)* that get the boy dead right. Right at the start, Kemble shows Huck in a cleaner line drawing in an almost identical pose as Williams; except here, the boy is holding a dead rabbit by its legs like a lantern in one hand, and the barrel of a shotgun in another. He is more improbably wearing shoes here and his attire—one suspender holding up his 'grown man's trousers'—is less shambolic. He is staring right at us with a triumphant smile; after all, in *Huckleberry Finn* he is also the narrator.

But if there is one image that captures everything about Huck Finn it is Kemble's singular one captioned 'Taking a Rest'.

Free bird: *EW Kemble's illustration from 'The Adventures of Huckleberry Finn (Tom Sawyer's Companion)', Mark Twain, 1884*

Twain's corresponding text is stunning by the sheer description of what Huck sees:

> I got out amongst the driftwood, and then laid down in the bottom of the canoe and let it float. I laid there, and had a good rest and a smoke out of my pipe, looking away into the sky; not a cloud in it. The sky looks ever so deep when you lay down on your back in the moonshine; I never knowed it before.

With Kemble's picture, though, it is almost unnecessary. Seeing Huck, pipe in hand, smoke rising out of his mouth, utterly free while ironically cabined, cribbed, canoed there on the river, one *sees* freedom.

It is the cover illustration of the 1959 Signet Classic edition by an uncredited artist (Bernie Fuchs?), however, that captures Huck's hangdog independence perfectly. He is seen sitting on the edge of a wooden bank next to reeds, his dungarees rolled up and feet in the Mississippi, looking straight at us half-defiantly, half-curiously, one hand holding a lit pipe, with the opposite bank and civilisation in the background. We can see the man that lies barely under the surface of this boy constantly hurried into grown-up life. He already looks rested. (The corresponding cover of *Tom Sawyer* by the same artist depicts an unruly boy holding a wooden sword and smiling at us. It is a boy who looks like someone given enough time and space to live out his boyhood at a normal pace. He looks restless.)

Boy overboard: *Cover of the 1959 Signet Classic edition of 'Adventures of Huckleberry Finn,' artist unknown*

In Dashu's case, despite Sukumar Ray being an accomplished illustrator having drawn numerous drawings accompanying his nonsense verse and stories, there is none of Pagla Dashu in his hand. The illustrations he drew to accompany two of the four Dashu stories—'Chinepotka' (Chinese Crackers) and 'Dashur Kirti' ('Dashu's Deed')—both depict the boy's two most famous stunts, but not the boy. The first illustration shows a startled teacher in mid-flight with tumbling furniture, and the second has a person covering the head of a victim with a sack, Guantanamo Bay-style, with another chap creeping up with a pichkadi to finish off the dastardly act. Neither of the youngsters in the second picture depicts Dashorothi.

For that, we have to go to the 1940 Signet Press edition of *Pagla Dashu*, a collection of 20 Sukumar Ray's stories of which 16 are 'non-Dashu'. The illustrations of Dashorothi by Sukumar's son Satyajit of Apu-Mukul-Piku fame, capture the librarylooniness, the irreverence and iconoclastic nature of the boy. In the most famous image that makes the cover is a smiling Dashu, turning around with an impish smile and shock of hair, eyes brimming with a rule-destroying plan. It is the same mischievous look that can be found, when sought, in some grown-ups like Uttam Kumar in his romantic comedies like the 1953 *Sharey Chuattor* (Seventy-Four and a Half) and 1954 *Ora Thake Odhare* (They Live That Side).

High loon: *Cover illustration by Satyajit Ray of 'Pagla Dashu' (Signet Press), Sukumar Ray, 1940*

But the portrait of Dashu that gives an inkling of a future Dashorothi-babu is Satyajit's rendition of Sukumar's description of the boy making a political statement in the first story:

> Once he suddenly appeared in school wearing a pair of trousers. Wearing trousers that looked like floppy pajamas and a coat that was like a pillow cover, the fact that he looked exceedingly odd, he himself understood. And that he was looking odd by itself was giving him much pleasure. We asked, 'Why are you wearing trousers?' He smiled and said, 'So that I can learn English well.'

Counter-cultural: *Satyajit Ray's illustration from 'Pagla Dashu'*

The usual dhoti-shirt-clad Dashu appears smug as a bug in Satyajit's drawing, books tucked under his arm, the Western clothes and shoes almost making him look like a proto-university mathematics/philosophy professor. Wittgenstein would have spoken if he had set his eyes on this image; he wouldn't have been silent.

***

So, where would these two startling kids have 'ended up' if they did come of age—as if adulthood is a destination of some sort? Sukumar Ray didn't leave any Dashu DNA trail behind to reverse (forward?) engineer him as an adult. The last mention of him in any work is: 'Well, is Dashu *really* really mad, or does he just fake it?'

Twain, though, certainly followed through with the thought, even if only in an authorial plan. In the conclusion to *Tom Sawyer*, he wrote:

> So endeth this chronicle. It being strictly a history of a boy, it must stop here; the story could not go much further without becoming the history of a man. When one writes a novel about grown people, he knows exactly where to stop—that is, with a marriage; but when he writes of juveniles, he must stop where he best can.

Most of the characters that perform in this book still live, and are prosperous and happy. Some day it may seem worth while to take up the story of the younger ones again and see what sort of men and women they turned out to be; therefore it will be wisest not to reveal any of that part of their lives at present.

Huck does continue as narrator and character in Twain's 1894 book *Tom Sawyer Abroad* and the 1896 *Tom Sawyer, Detective*. But like Hergé's Tintin and Satyajit Ray's Feluda adventures, these books are about other things: (parodies of) adventure and detective novels of that time. Huck does not grow and we never know Mr Finn. All the teaser of a clue we are left with is the last two sentences in *Huckleberry Finn*:

> Tom's most well now; and got his bullet around his neck on a watch-guard for a watch, and is always seeing what

> time it is, and so there ain't nothing more to write about, and I am rotten glad of it, because if I'd a knowed what a trouble it was to make a book I wouldn't a tackled it, and ain't a-going to no more. But I reckon I got to light out for the Territory ahead of the rest, because Aunt Sally she's going to adopt me and sivilize me, and I can't stand it. I been there before.

There is a reason for Twain wondering about his creation as a grown-up. After initially denying that he was based on any real person, Twain did admit that Huckleberry Finn, unlike Tom Sawyer or any other of his characters, was based on a boy he once knew. When Twain was still a boy named Samuel L. Clemens, he was friends with a local boy in Hannibal, Missouri, Tom Blankenship. In his autobiography—a ramble of recollections as any unedited, true autobiography should be—Twain wrote/said:

> In 'Huckleberry Finn' I have drawn Tom Blankenship exactly as he was. He was ignorant, unwashed, insufficiently fed; but he had as good a heart as ever any boy had. His liberties were totally unrestricted. He was the only really independent person—boy or man—in the community, and by consequence, he was tranquilly and continuously happy and envied by the rest of us. And as his society was forbidden us by our parents the prohibition trebled and quadrupled its value, and therefore we sought and got more of his society than any other boy's.

This Tom's father was indeed a vicious drunkard. This Tom was indeed free and 'enjoyed' neglect.

Huckleberry, being in his early teens in the Antebellum period and in his late 30s when the US Civil War began in 1861, would have most certainly been sought and drafted as a Confederate soldier for cannon fodder, unless he managed to dodge the conflated 'sivilizing' grip of Aunt Sally and Society. He could still have found himself 'died' after having taken to the bottle like his pap, and slipped into TS Eliot's 'strong brown god' of a river, a sacrifice for the life of utter liberation he lived.

Or, as is quite possible with an ingenious lad, he may have wised up enough as a young man, bartered himself into some money, given up the outcast romantic/antisocial degenerate life to run a business in pelt. Much like Rimbaud relinquished his youth of poetry and absinthe, and turning his back on when 'our mad heart goes Crusoeing through all the romances' when one is seventeen, to become a trader in coffee and arms in Aden, Yemen, and later Harar, Ethiopia (the very same year Twain's *Huckleberry Finn* was published). Perhaps, Albert Camus would have also targeted Finn for committing 'spiritual suicide' and becoming a 'bourgeois trafficker'.

If he survived the turn of the century, Finn would have been in his late 70s, when life expectancy for White men in America was 46.6 years. It is impossible to imagine him with family. If St Petersburg couldn't tame him when he was free to be free, a wife and child would certainly not have brought the same comfort as a pelt trade enterprise. Which, knowing his normalisation of being pelted and brutally beaten by his own father, may be just as well.

Dashorothi's future as a young man, then a middle-aged man, and finally as an old man, may seem more secure, more 'in the script'. Perhaps an Apu-like settling down is not only believable, but even inevitable. But the longer you linger, the more possible it is that a character goes out of character. The golden rule of real life may be 'past behaviour determines future behaviour,' but there is always context and chronology to contend with.

If Dashorothi was around twelve in 1916, he would have been around four when Khudiram Bose was hanged at age 18 in 1908. Going into school—the only place we have met him, and we know that children can behave very differently at home—he must have been aware of the cult of the martyr teenager. By the time Dashu himself is eighteen, Chauri Chaura occurs, Mohandas Gandhi is arrested and then sentenced for sedition.

Does Dashu have a violent bone in his body? Sukumar Ray wouldn't have told us even if he did, since *his* boy was a sharp, unruly kid who disliked authority and injustice in school. The world, of course, was, and remains, a very different place. But how different? When does a prank about egging on greedy classmates to open a lunch box that upon opening is found to be empty except for a taunting note, 'Eat kachkola!' (the equivalent of 'Eat this!') and 'Too much curiosity is not good', metamorphose into acts considered seditious against real authority figures of a colonial regime? When does a claypot full of Chinese crackers that scares the class teacher shitless out of his chair turn into chucking bombs at symbols of repression or armoury raids? Or, for that matter when does breaking rules as a boy metastasise into causing genuine harm to others, as a man.

They may well not have at all. Dashorothi may well have been enthused by the discoveries at Mohenjodaro by Kashinath Narayan Dikshit and John Marshall in the mid-1920s and found himself a position of excavatory study and scholarship in the Archaeological Survey of India. The chances of him settling and resettling can only be answered by the last question asked by Sukumar Ray's narrator about him: 'Is Dashu *really* really mad, or does he just fake it?'

Depression may not have taken a romantic turn in the middle-aged man if Dashorothi-babu found himself labouring under nostalgia and living out a banal life. For a boy so self-aware, a voyant-voyou—seer-mischief-maker—being in denial would hardly be an option for the man. As for his penchant for pranks, the cause for such joy in his boyhood, would he have continued to seek justice by overturning established orders and dogmas after years of finding out that things slide back to their own sense of triteness? How would Dashu, age 50, reckon with surf unerringly turning back into water no matter how much he churned the sea? In his case too then, we find a possibility of a real boy (whom everybody knows) who did go on to become a real man (whom nobody cares to know).

The 66-year-old Ernest Delahaye, writing in his 1919 memoir, *Delahaye, Témoin de Rimbaud* (Delahaye, Witness to Rimbaud) recalls his then-18-year-old childhood *school* friend

Arthur Rimbaud—who would have been (a respectable?) 65 if he had been alive when the book was published—confiding in him in 1872:

> It's so annoying. I have a terrible reputation in Paris now. Reasons: friends' pranks, and also my own, moreover. I thought it would be fun—it was stupid—to pass myself off as an ignoble pig. They would take me at my word. One day, I tell them that I went to [composer Ernest] Cabaner's room while he was out and found a glass of milk that had been poured for him; that I jerked off into it, that I ejaculated into it. They laughed about it, and they went around repeating it as though it were true.

But onward blithe spirit of permanent boyhood. The fallacy of foisting future tragedy on fictional boys is as silly as being hoisted on one's own petard. So, it would be best to let Dashu and Huck spend the rest of their fictional lives in the most cabined of classrooms and narrowest of canoes that still-life in page-turning narrative can device.

I would think that Rana by now, too, has become a figment of imagination, a boy that will never reach adulthood in a variation of Zeno's 'Achilles and the Tortoise' paradox. Which is just as well. For you see, all old people have been young. But not all young people have been old. Or need be.

WHY I AM NOT A MISO SOUP

One of the more interesting features of casual drinking is the benderangement of words the drinker hears. This Pnohm Penhomenon also happens to be the least investigated part of investigations into drunkenness. Which doesn't surprise me, considering the curious mind of the sober investigator encounters far louder, far more attention-seeking standing-under-the-streetlights features in a person whose blood alcohol concentration is sloshing at around 0.266%—meaning that there is .266g of alcohol for every 100 ml of blood. Which is much more than you think it is, and I once thought it to be.

I have been blessed with such mishearings, however, much before I ever started drinking. I still listen to the chorus of the Michael Jackson song in my head (I never play it aloud) that goes 'You wanna be startin' somethin'/

You got to be startin' somethin' as 'I wanna be a dinosaur/ I gotta be a dinosaur'. Or the forgotten, less famous song that I would hear as a kid that no amount of Google searching now can make me find the 'original' version of, whose lines I have bent into BDSM shape to be,

'Blue shadows in the night/ Dracula and the werewolf come alive/ [unintelligble] where the waters go/ [unintelligble, unintelligble, unintelligble]'. Let's just say the original is a Christian hymn of some sorts.

I still think by mishearing the lines, 'She said,/ In the days when you were hopelessly poor/ I just liked you more' as 'She said,/ In the days when you were hopelessly *bored*/ I just liked you more', I actually improved Morissey's lyrics of the Smiths' song, 'Half a Person'. True, I *may* have been projecting.

The rather unscientific-sounding scientific term for this activity is mondegreen, a rare occasion when a term itself is an example of what it is. It came about when Sylvia Wright, a writer and former editor of *Harper's Bazaar* coined the term in her 1954 essay, 'The Death of Lady Mondegreen'. She described how as a child, she would listen to her mother reading aloud from Thomas Percy's 1765 *Reliques of Ancient English Poetry* one of her favourite poems that began, 'Ye Highlands and ye Lowlands,/ Oh, where hae ye been?/ They hae slain the Earl Amurray/ And Lady Mondegreen.' The last line of this stanza from the ballad, The Bonnie Earl o'Murray, 'And laid him on the green,' is magically transformed, thereby stopping Earl o'Murray from being left, in Wright's words, 'to die all alone without even anyone to hold his hand—I won't have it'.

Did this woman have to die? Really? *Illustration from Sylvia Wright's 'The Death of Lady Mondegreen', Bernarda Bryson, Harper's Magazine, November 1954*

Drinking, in its most serious format of lightening up life that is undeniably scabby, invites such cognitive dissonance—thereby making people instinctively make *their* own sense of something that they can't comprehend. And my list of things I can't comprehend is staggeringly long. Thus, the puzzling desire to be a dinosaur or the discovery of a vampiric-lycanic compact (or conflict?) much before the *Underworld* movies made their mutual hostility a pop cultural trope. Or find it more High Romantic to be bored than to be poor.

As Stephen Pinker—the cognitive psychologist, whom I constantly mis-see as Simon Rattle, former conductor of the Berlin Philharmonic because of their hair and face-cut—writes in *The Language Instinct*,

> The interesting thing about mondegreens is that the mis-hearings are generally *less* plausible than the intended lyrics. In no way do they bear out any sane listener's general expectations of what a speaker is likely to say or

> mean...Apparently, listeners lock in to some set of words that fit the sound and that hang together more or less as English words and phrases [it works with non-English words and phrases too, Stephen Rattle!] but plausibility and general expectations are not running the show.

So what *is* running the show? Just rando substitutions with rampant homophonia suddenly emerging when the brain fails to process the speaker's Nintended words? Like the time an army general from the defence agency funding a Carnegie-Mellon University artificial intelligence programme in the 1970s, HEARSAY, which moved chess pieces on the board according to speech perceptions, cleared his throat and the programme printed, 'Pawn to King 4'? Mesa don't think so.

For natural intelligence, the randomness has the spit and cough of our mental innards shaped by our experiences, thrown into that René Go-Fuck-Yourself Descartesian cauldron. Or so I would like to believe considering that beliefs and thinking in this case are always post facto, like a chap trying to figure out why a girl slept with him only *after* the sleeping has been done. What we mishear is, I fervently believe, determined by what we are as individual sentient sponge bobs.

Why else would the (since discredited) pioneer of 'subliminal advertising' James Vickery tell the brewery company he was hired by in the 1950s not to use the word 'lagered'—adj. intoxicated, esp after drinking lager—after his (since discredited) study found that even though a third of his survey respondents associated 'lagered' with 'beer', another third associated it with tiredness, dizziness and laggardness? One theory I am ready to believe has it that Vickery didn't like the word himself, so concocted the result of his study accordingly. But you know what I'm saying about words and how we deal with t**m.

So, the most enigmatic of all my mondegreens has to be one that I will care to explain, armed as I am with my understanding of why I think what I think—which is like holding a switchblade while facing Godzilla's descending and fused metatarsals. The fact that I had had a few glasses of plonk—Beaujolais in a carafe in the northern French town of Lille, no less—only provides a context.

Now, Lille is a lovely town with a lovely train station that has a fountain in front of its entrance. Let me loose in a lovely town with a lovely station that has a fountain in front of its entrance and I am bound to let my hair—and the chaperone from my publishing company—down. Which I did. In a press meet that was palpably 20th-century where I, along with a few other writers, were being asked questions about our latest novels, the most interesting one that came my way was, 'Are you a miso soup?' Which, this being the hometown of the 13th-century poet Jacquemart Giélée—whose update on Reynard the Fox in 8,048 verses has a lioness and a leopardess have a qawwali fight over a fox—I had to treat as a valid question.

Now, as far as I go, my association with France and the literature that goes under the rubric of Francophonic is special. I say Francophonic and not French because I do consider the chorus line of the song by the New York band Les Têtes Parlantes—'Qu'est-ce que c'est/

Fa-fa-fa-fa-fa-fa-fa-fa-fa-far better'—to be right up there with authentic maal contents like Rabelais' 'Je m'en vais chercher un grand peut-être' (I am going to seek a great perhaps) and Eric Cantona's 'When the seagulls follow the trawler, it's because they think sardines will be thrown into the sea.' (Quand les mouettes suivent le chalutier, c'est parce qu'elles pensent que les sardines vont être jetées à la mer). In other words, I appreciate the French way without really understanding it.

I had decided before the press engagement that I would tank up on copious litres of red wine, ensure that I mutter into my microphone from time to time the word 'Merde' in an antipodal and, therefore, complementary manner to the way Rimbaud had once shouted 'Merde!' at the end of every line recited by every poet—one of whom he managed to stab and injure—at a poetry reading session. So there I was, Rimbaudelaired to my gills and quivering to my tits facing the query, 'Are you a miso soup?', which, to be fair, came with the pretext (or is it context?) that I had a habit of killing off/maiming the female characters in my novels.

On the face of it, it was a fair point. In one of my novels, I had ended the book with the woman on whose discovery the whole story was plotted not existing at all—a fact which my publisher, the bidi-chainsmoking, cleanshaven Gandalf Ravi Dayal thought fit to put in the book's blurb right at the beginning, and rightly, since it's not *what* you keep under your sleeve that matters but *how*. In another novel, I had one of the main (male) characters dowse a mosquito net with kerosene and burn a woman, his girlfriend, sleeping inside it, and the other (male) protagonist be pushed by a woman to his death through a window. And in yet another book, I had one woman puked upon in a moving train and the other go into a coma, although I do let on quickly enough that she is faking the coma for tactical, empowering reasons.

It can be, with the evidence available, hard to prove that I am a miso soup. Harder still to prove that I'm not. But as you may have guessed, the lady asking me the question was not curious about whether or not I considered myself to be a dashi stock mixed with fermented soya beans and koji. Instead, she wanted to know whether I was a misogynist—a lady-killer, a man who dislikes women, a vagino-Fagin, a femalcontent. In the Beaujolais smog in which the spirit of D'artagnan had d'escended on me like Venus fastens on her prey, I parried this query initially in my own head, convinced that, no, I was not, and never would be, a miso soup. Chholar (chana) daal maybe, when pushed into a corner, but miso soup, never. 'Merde,' I said, before I grasped—'chose to grasp' being more honest and accurate—the journalist's true question.

As far as the theory of mondegreens as adaptive protective devices go, saying 'misogynist' and hearing 'miso soup' sounds a stretch, even by dinosaur-cosplaying standards. But there it was. A question that I could only ignore to my own dismay. So, after another string of 'merdes', this time more self-effacingly Jerry Lewis than ambitiously Rimbaud, I attempted to clear my name and simultaneously the air. My novels are not brimming with characters like a Netflix novel. So, when I do bump off people—and I do absolutely need to for the sake of form, if not plot—my erasures are gender-agnostic. I have made a male character disappear (permanently) into an uncovered manhole. I have, as earlier mentioned, bumped off another man via defenestration. And when there are deaths of women—my women don't do SOP heartbreak—they are quite noble, Brunhilda to the breed.

I said all this, convincingly to my ear, not so persuasively to the feedback from my microphone that I still remember howling like a laughter in electric.

Now, minus beaujolais and Le Mondegreen, without performance anxiety and armed with Pantosil, I can safely, honestly tell you, I am not a miso soup. Having grown up in a household overwhelmingly manned by women, any ability to distinguish the abilities of men from women—barring in the most obvious, superficial ways—has disappeared in proportion to my ability to treat everyone—man, woman, child, cricket stump—as equal, except in intelligence, where the division of the goodies is not gender-based but randomised. Any nervousness I feel in the presence of a woman, especially an attractive woman, I feel because of the most, obvious, superficial reasons. Although, it must be said that like any anti-Muslim, anti-semitic, racist or classist bigot, I am able to discriminate—in the sense of perceiving differences—women from men instinctively, like some folks are magically able to tell whether a man is carrying beef in a tiffin carrier or chicken. I am too old now to be unable to discriminate between the multiplying sexes, although I have indeed made a mistake a couple of times.

If there is a whiff of misogyny in me, it is because of the disappointment some women evoke in me when they believe themselves to be inferior to men. I hold or slam the door behind me for men and women alike, depending on how much I dislike them as individuals. As a 'class,' women are prettier men.

In fact, some of my best friends are women. I will, though, kill or at least seriously maim more male characters in my stories from now on. Merde.

FELUMENON, A BHADRALOK FRANCHISE

This is not about Feluda, the intrepid private investigator created by Satyajit Ray, and for which more people know the great filmmaker than for his (non-Feluda, internationally acclaimed) movies. This is about the Feluda 'phenomenon', or, as I'd like to call it, the Felumenon.

But to go any further, it is necessary to traipse along a bit about what amounts to being a 'phenomenon,' a word that shoots out various meanings that are tenuously connected. Stopping by Immanuel Kant's version on a Khan Market autumn evening, one recognises a phenomenon as anything that can be observed by the senses and, therefore, worthy of investigation. This, understandably, is also the meaning that science gives to phenomena.

A shade apart is 'phenomenon' to describe an unusual or untoward event. Its usage for 'unnatural' events or things—in the sense of what can't be explained with reason, such as UFOs, the Yeti, spontaneous human combustion, visitations of the dead, the Electral sex appeal of Narendra Modi—is to be noted, considering we now find the term used for both observable matters and those whose observation is patchy, iffy and spectral.

A more modern usage of phenomenon is in the sense of something or (usually) someone who stands out from the crowd. Joan Baez used it in this sense in her thinly veiled song about her old flame Bob Dylan in 'Diamonds and Rust': 'Well, you burst on the scene/ Already a legend/ The unwashed phenomenon'. The more prosaic (over)usage of the term comes in the form of 'phenomenal,' usually accompanied by an exclamation mark, to denote something remarkable and exceptionally good—such a 'phenomenal run rate' or 'phenomenal ability to remember'.

It is in this radial—and radiating—view of the word that I approach Felumenon.

Satyajit Ray wrote 35 Feluda stories, the first in 1965 when Lal Bahadur Shastri was prime minister, the last in 1992 when PV Narasimha Rao was in office. Ray made two Feluda movies: the 1971 novel *Sonar Kella* (The Golden Fortress) in 1974, and the 1975 *Joy Baba Felunath* (All Hail Felunath) in 1979. Most of the stories were first consumed by readers in the children's magazines *Sandesh* and *Anandamela*, especially in the latter's Durga Puja annuals. These *adventure* novels fitted perfectly with the annual Puja spirit—of venturing out to new locales, with a mystery wrapping these journeys.

Ray's two Feluda films not only gave flesh to these stories, but also took the viewer 'out there': Rajasthan, in the case of *Sonar Kella*; Varanasi, in the case of *Joy Baba Felunath*. Like Hergé's Adventures of Tintin, the Adventures of Feluda in film were as much visual forays into places as they were about a smart—borderline smart-ass—man solving mysteries.

Ray's two Feluda films are also as much about the dialogues as they are about the stories. In fact, I'd say their iconic appeal is due to the comedic lines of the character of Lalmohan Ganguly, the writer of alliteratively titled pulp thrillers under the nom de plume Jatayu. Lalmohan's lines from the movies form a part of contemporary Bengali pop culture, memorised wholesale by Feluda fans and recalled like song lyrics by pretty much everyone else. They are also almost always lost in English translation. The Feluda films, too, are the least translatable, being the most tied to the 'Bengali' urban context, of his movies. And it is this particularity that doesn't travel beyond the Bengali umma that gives Felumenon its thump.

But as with any goose able to lay golden eggs, Felumenon was put on the conveyor belt almost immediately after Ray's death in 1992. His son, Sandip, has been churning out television and cinematic dramatisations of Feluda stories since 1996 when, as part of two packages for Doordarshan Bangla—'Feluda 30' and 'Satyajiter Goppo' (Satyajit's Tales)—the 1972 novel, *Baksho Rahashya* (Mystery of the Box) was dramatised. Sandip's last Feluda film, *Hatyapuri* (House of Murder/Murderous Puri) based in Puri, once *the* seaside vacation go-to place for Bengalis in coastal Odisha, was released in 2022. With Indraneil Sengupta as Felu, this relatively understated film is actually one I have enjoyed the most in decades.

PC Mitter & Co. Unltd: *Poster of TV Series, 'Feluda Pherot' renamed, 'Feludar Goyendagiri', 2020, dir. Srijit Mukherji, Addatimes*

Others have taken a stab at Feluda-filming, and certainly will continue to do so till Howrah freezes over. Shabash Feluda (Hooray Feluda), was released three days after the '102nd Birth Anniversary of Ray', the director is quoted reminding everyone. To get into the good, bad and fugliness of these television shows, films, streaming series is as pointless as an invitation to a trap. The films themselves from the Feluda factory are secondary. Like Rajinikanth movies, it doesn't matter whether they are good or bad; they will be watched, discussed, compared, used as diving boards for more Feluda franchise. In other words, this mandatory following on Felu feeds the Felumenon at the altar of that Bengali god, Satyajit Ray.

***

The bhadralok in the Bengali universe is the genteel man imbued with a certain set of characteristics like a phone preloaded with certain apps. These include a certain taciturnity, knowledge of the demonstrable kind, a respectable lack of ambition, but above all, respecting the value of these characteristics even when not necessarily having them.

Feluda, a.k.a. Prodosh C. Mitter, an Anglicisation of the Bengali Mitra, is a prototype of this 20th-century bhadralok. His measured words, always in response to the situation or the garrulous Lalmohan Ganguly, are supposed to be the tip of the iceberg that lies above his repository of knowledge. Even in the post-Google world, Felu easily impresses by making connections that are not apparent to anyone else: some Sanskrit word that provides a clue; some shadowy figure in history that leads to a solution; some small dialecticle difference in the use of a word; some bookish knowledge about a location that allows him to push on. Lalmohanbabu, like the middle-class non-bhadralok Bengali, finds such a repository of information and processor of knowledge astounding, someone worth 'cultivating'.

Feluda's lack of ambition—he seems to take on cases that fancy him or pique his interest, rather than depending on professional private investigation as a livelihood—is seen as laudable by the Bengali middle class. It mirrors the respect they set aside for those not driven by economic well/better-being. The disdain for those who are money-minded—the swindlers and smugglers, most notably the iconic Maganlal Meghraj, a Marwari who epitomises the Bengali's disdain for these wealth-creators and their 'lack of culture' despite (because of?) keeping 'Bengali' Kolkata afloat by their enterprise—somehow does not apply to miserly Bengalis. A certain thread of condescension on Feluda's part runs through the stories and films as far as his best-selling writer and biggest fan Jatayu is concerned, and it's not only because of the latter's lack of research and knowledge which he demonstrates frequently, like the information bumpkin that he is, but also because he is 'successful'.

In this Felu worldview, worldly success and greed are interchangeable, almost synonyms. His quip against Lalmohan-babu's loud, flashy new green car is the bhadralok's derision of money. A derision that is usually possible by being financially comfortable oneself.

It is in this giant vat of constantly updated versions of 20th-century bhadralokness that a suave (but not too suave), Bengali (but atypical Bengali) Christ cleansing the Temple, is presented like a Passion play to the mob.

In no other culture is a pop cultural hero so aspirationally distant from his worshippers, not even Sherlock, with his digressions of violin, cocaine and beekeeping. In his 1988 book, *Atyoghati Bangali* (The Suicidal Bengali), Niradchandra Chaudhuri—no less than a Commander of the Most

Excellent Order of the British Empire (CBE) along with the likes of Joan Collins—wrote: 'The authentic Bengali has a habit—he thinks of himself as extremely intelligent, but never realises that however he may consciously think of himself, in actuality that is not true, because he is merely clever, not intelligent.'

It is by gladly collapsing the two—clever and intelligent—that new Feluda productions fulfil the demand that the Avengers franchise of movies and shows provide for another thrill-seeking clientele. The real reason for Ray's own two Feluda films striking such a chord with transgenerational middle-class Bengali audiences is not because of the hero played by Soumitra 'Apu' Chatterjee, but the presence of Lalmohan Ganguly, Nirad Chaudhuri's 'authentic' Bengali. Played in both movies by Santosh Dutta with such aplomb that Ray rightly decided not to make another Feluda film after Dutta's death in 1988. After *Sonar K*ella, Ray even incorporated Dutta's mannerisms and look in his Felu stories and the illustrations accompanying them.

It is in this rotund, balding, easily impressed, easily scared, vacation-loving, always shocked, always awed middle-class man that the Bengali recognises himself in the Ray Feluda movies. In subsequent productions, he is what he only in theory is: a moddhyobitto (middle-class) comic foil to the gravitas-drenched dashing bhadralok hero.

But the crank keeps turning, Feluda movies keep churning out, the churn itself becoming a part of contemporary Bengali popular culture to be looked forward to every year; to be taken to the cleaners (itself a joyous activity) or positively rated next to the pair of Golden Yardsticks of Ray's *Shonar Kella* and *Joy Baba Felunath*.

The films are all tailored to OTT viewing—in both senses of aesthetic and technological over-the-top—and don't provide the subtle montages or change of frames that gave Ray's dramatisations of his stories such a subliminal power. Instead of the faux Rorschach Test cards that those movies provide the Bengali viewer, the new ones are almost literal visualisations of Ray's stories. And most tellingly, the dialogues—'Apni ki shuor?' (Are you a pig? [upon hearing Felu's chest-waist measurements of 26–26 inches]), 'Highly sussspicccious!' or 'Hajar hajar Hajra' ([There] are thousands of Hajras), or the knife-throwing scene in Joy Baba Felunath, or the muscles-flexing one in the same movie—are absent by being bloodless in the new movies. Or overdone, in the sense of making competitive bids to outdo Lalmohan babooisms, and ending up with full-on buffoonery. This is because directors, devotees of Ray's Feluda movies and stories reaching out to fellow devotees, are wont to inject their own non-visual touches in the script, the very aspect that Ray moved away from in his own stories to work on his dialogue-writing craft without fear or favour.

Felumenon feeds and feeds off the Feluda Industry. It provides Bengali cinema's producers and consumers a steady drip with a return on investment that is assured no matter what the reviews say. It also provides a hall of mirrors inside the larger frog well where the Bengali holds on to this otherwise precarious version of Bengaliness—the bhadralok private investigator where both bhadralok behaviour and honest detection are becoming rarer than a self-effacing politician.

Feluda® has long joined the equal-part nostalgic, equal-part aspirational Fauxeux tapestry: Calcutta's glory (sic) during the British era when it was the capital of a country and not just a BIMARU-W state; Calcutta's throbbing metropolitanism in the 1960s with its Park Street nightclubs and music; Calcutta's revolutionary zeitgeist in the 1970s during the Naxal agitation, itself a hark-back to the early 20th century when the city was the theatre of anti-colonial 'revolutionaries', the intellectual and cultural capital of the universe...

Felumenon's singular appeal today is providing glimpses of what 'could have been' with Bengalis, with Bengal, with Kolkata, as a foil to—and sanctuary from—'India'.

In 1843, Charles Dickens published *A Christmas Carol* where readers were introduced to the Ghosts of Christmas Past, of Christmas Present and of Christmas Yet to Come. In 1882, Bankimchandra Chattopadhyay, who was sure to have read the English writer's Christmas special, published *Anandamath* where readers were introduced to the Mother(land) 'as she was', 'as she now is' and 'as she shall be'. Ray's Feluda films, still dipped into with fervour and fun on OTT platforms and YouTube, evokes the Bengali as he was, not is, but hopefully will be. It is something one holds on to for dear civilisational life with solace and hope So, why on earth would anyone want to kick this habit?

EVERYBODY LOVES A GOOD MOURNING

Public deaths redeem my faith in humanity. Which is significantly different from public deaths making me believe in the innate goodness of humans. That, unfortunately, would be kidding myself the way I still kid myself into believing that the world's first heavy metal song, 'Helter Skelter', was sung by any Beatle other than Paul for the simple reason that I find him rather pasty. What makes me respect humans immediately after the death of a popular figure is that for the duration of collective mourning, they become empathic to otherwise elusive private sorrow. Even telepathic, to an extent.

The death of a person is serious business. And it is extremely hard to share in the seriousness of the ending of a life when the world not only goes on, but goes on in full gusto. In all the squelching out of breath, flattened monopitch of a flatline, shelling of bodies—never understood why 'shelling peas' isn't '*de*shelling peas'—traffic, sex, school, shopping, eating continue without dropping a beat. After the deaths of persons, that is. As the king cliché goes, life goes on, dancing around the maypole of a life that actually doesn't go on. It's almost as if the original word for life was 'ath,' and *de*ath is the opposite of it. De-ath.

Quite famously, this sentiment of the world refusing to stop to take note, never mind a minute's silence, of a death is captured by Pieter Bruegel the Elder's circa 1560 painting, Landscape With the Fall of Icarus; the attribution to Bruegel Sr has been considered 'doubtful' since a study was conducted on the painting in 1996. But then, with so much in doubt, I'd like to believe that both, WH Auden and William Carlos Williams who wrote about the same painting, would have approved and disapproved at the same time Icarus's fall not making a splash on primetime news, which is all the time, anytime.

For Auden, in his 1907 poem, 'Musée des Beaux Art,'

'...everything turns away
Quite leisurely from the disaster; the ploughman may
Have heard the splash, the forsaken cry,
But for him it was not an important failure; the sun shone
As it had to on the white legs disappearing into the green
Water, and the expensive delicate ship that must have seen
Something amazing, a boy falling out of the sky,
Had somewhere to get to and sailed calmly on.'

There is no Planet-B: *'Landscape With the Fall of Icarus' c. 1560, commonly attributed to Pieter Bruegel the Elder*

This is the world of hypobole, the opposite of our hyperbolic one where everything is not just underwhelming, but everyone is underwhelmed even by 'something amazing' like a meteor-boy. Icarus, cocky and brimming with hubris has his own bildungsroman:

- From meteroid ('not to be confused with meteorite'), a small body in outer space travelling at about 42 km/sec escape velocity from the Sun
- Then to meteor ('not to be confused with meteroid'), the visible rite of passage of a meteroid glowing from friction in the Earth's atmosphere
- Finally to meteorite ('not to be confused with meteor'), a portion of the meteroid that hits the ground or water without being destroyed after passing through

> the Earth's atmosphere. Which would at least be Icarus's 'white legs' going by Bruegel's depiction.

While the very overdressed farmer in the foreground ploughs without distraction, and a shabby shepherd with his dog next to him and tending to his sheep looks up,perhaps upon hearing the sonic boom created by the flailing Icarus's legs, it is the ship closest to the shore that seems to have been nearest the plunging boy after the angler who is too busy fishing to look up.

Peering into Pieter-saab's painting, one can see a sailor clambering up the running line, another straddled across the ship's spar, in the process of releasing the sheet, while a couple of others seem busy on the crow's nest. Now consider Phlebus being the name of the sailor climbing up the running line on the ship in Bruegel's painting. By William Carlos Williams's punctilious, punctuationless reckoning in his 1960 poem, 'Landscape with the Fall of Icarus':

'...the edge of the sea
concerned
with itself

sweating in the sun
that melted
the wings' wax

unsignificantly
off the coast
there was

a splash quite unnoticed
this was
Icarus drowning'

Williams's is a news bulletin, in today's buzzphrasekill language 'BREAKING NEWS' of the world as media-tor, ignoring this iconic drowning. 'Unsignificance' is smeared on this tragedy, 'a splash quite unnoticed'. This is not Nature's savoir faire in action, anthropomorphic humanity shown its place in the larger picture of sun and sea, but apathy. Of Nature, of man, which the media-tor seeks to correct.

Which is why consider Phlebus, the possible sailor nearest Icarus on the ship, whom TS Eliot in his 1922 'The Waste Land' introduces us as already a fortnight dead. In the 'Death by Water' section of the poem, we learn that Phlebus was a Phoenician, so from the eastern Mediterranean, probably modern CNN-worthy, Christiane Amanpoured Lebanon. We also learn that he

'Forgot the cry of gulls, and the deep sea swell
And the profit and loss.'

Eliot isn't talking about the sailor in the Bruegel painting where an older drowning is happening as if caught on someone's mobile phone camera but not 'on news'. I am. Because if Phlebus ignored the struggling splashes of a drowning man even as he was in eyeshot if not in ear—he was high enough and near enough to have seen the tumult and the waters churn—did he mark himself to the gods to be dead by water too? Could he have dived in and attempted to save the waxed Icarus from his watery, presumably still boiling death? Instead, did he help the 'expensive delicate ship' that 'had somewhere to get to and sailed calmly on' and thereby seal his own death by water?

Hot Legs: *Detail from 'Landscape With the Fall of Icarus'*

It is the oddity of news as we consume it now that comes ALL CAPS, is consumed ALL CAPS and yet, because of the loudness and all-pervasiveness of it, makes us relatively meh to it than ever before. Like the way a homeless family on a sidewalk in Kolkata and a gaggle of nudists on the banks of a Munich lake become invisible, so do every falling Icari elicit the same shrugged response whether it's 'something amazing, a boy falling out of the sky' or just rain.

And it is here where public sorrow, shared from a buffet table but consumed on a plate, is such an anomaly. I have not been part of any giant mourning assemblage. Not of actor-star Uttam Kumar in 1980, not of Indira Gandhi in 1984, not of Diana née Spencer Windsor in 1997, not of Diego Maradona in 2020. But the passing of public personalities does make the world seem filled with the heaviest of gases, grief, the response one usually expects to accompany every death (barring that of dictators, committers of heinous crimes and that sort).

The death of a popular, much- and many-loved person does make the ploughman, shepherd, Phlebus the Phoenician naval-gazer pause. Briefly, even if one doesn't join the mammoth funeral procession or participate in the national mourning, one senses the hum of hurt of a person's passing. The world, even if it doesn't stop, registers a loss, the traffic, traffic, sex, school, shopping, eating will at least seem unnatural. A multitude then feels what a few feel when their loved or admired one passes and *they* wonder why the multitude is numb to *their* grief.

When Rabindranath Tagore died in 1941, lakhs thronged to catch a glimpse of the passing body on the shoulders of standardbearers carrying the bamboo death stretcher.

The old British Movietone newsreel segment, captioned 'India Mourns Rabindranath Tagore,' (it was immediately followed by 'Eire Honours Parnell') captures the crowds in black and white, atomised, yet moving as a giant serpent through the streets of Calcutta as one gigantic, shared event.

What looks to uninitiated eyes like old wooden football rattles—the kind twirled by spectators in British football stands making a tribal kerkrackle until they were banned in the 1970s as they were used as handy weapons by football hooligans—were actually hand fans to momentarily unsettle the horrendous August humidity. In the footage, they flutter like moths in moth throes.

What was left out of the newsreel was the reported acts of mutilation of the much adored, great man's body. In *Tagore: The Myriad-Minded Man*, Krishna Dutta and Andrew Robinson write, 'As the funeral cortege moved haltingly along, hairs were plucked from the famous head, and at the cremation itself, besides the Ganges, before the body was completely burnt, the crowd invaded and began searching for bones and other relics of the poet's mortal being.' (In 2011, on Tagore's 100th death anniversary, a clutch of his beard was displayed in an exhibition at Dartington Hall at Totnes in Devon in Britain. The salt-and-pepper hair was apparently sent to Dartington by Tagore's son Rathindranath. But where did Rathindranath get it from? Which estate did Icarus's 'white legs disappearing into the green waters' end up at?)

Public death brings private grief home to people who

haven't tasted personal tragedy yet. It also gives us, for that brief while, an understanding of world sorrow, which, in turn, gives us a value of life (lower-cased). Every man is an island entire of itself; there is no continent, at best only archipelagos, where the Venn diagram crosses into one clutch of islands from another.

Crow's Nest: *Crowds wait to pay last respects as Mohandas Gandhi's funeral cortege approaches, New Delhi, 1948, Henri Cartier-Bresson, Magnum Photos*

Over the last couple of years, there have been too many deaths of people I have adored, I have loved, I have admired, I have known, along with people I have been familiar with. Some have been famous humans, others well-known—in the hierarchy of contemporary public valuation, there is a difference—and others whose work I knew about or whom I'd heard about from friends and family. These were not deaths by numbers; these were deaths by faces.

Facebook was the place where my archipelago congregated, writing a sermon, dredging a remembrance, literally posting our grief. Similarly, I saw other islands mourning the dead among their groups. While my death sorrow was strongest for *my* dead, seeing the dead of 'others' gave a kind of parity, a value to life that transcended familiarity.

And it's not only public deaths that make Bruegel's red tunic-clad farmer stop ploughing, the plodding shepherd look askance, all the sailors including phalse Phlebus stop working on the rig, the nonchalant angler closest to Icarus's flailing limb look up from his zen zone. The world stops when a great team loses, especially when so many humans have invested so much into believing they will win, and that they are great, and that they are impervious to humiliation. I was not alone when Germany crushed Argentina 4-0 in Cape Town in the 2010 World Cup quarterfinal. My archipelago mourned with me.

Which is not what I can say for the many defeats of other teams—one-person or otherwise—I support, the many deaths of people I have loved. The bloody traffic outside moves on as if not a splash was made in that greenish, ludicrously tranquil, lazy summer sunlit Aegean Sea.

THE PURGE A.K.A. THE DRY DAY

The prime function of a dry day—a day when the state doesn't allow you to purchase any alcoholic beverage from a retail store, and in many cases from any public house where liquor can be consumed—is to remind you of the importance of that day. And 'importance' takes on a very particular shade on such a day, that of sobriety, sombreness, respect of the kind that sees you not peek through closed eyes at a prayer meeting or crack knock-knock jokes at a sradh, or Narendra Modi sketches on a stand-up night. Which I did once at a friend's sradh—a Modi sketch, not a knock-knock joke. But the very close friends I was with knew that the departed, a very dear friend of mine, would have approved. So they smiled politely, even approvingly, in commiseration and did not hand me over to the Mobstapo.

We, drinkers, are usually armed and ready every 1 October, knowing that the next day will be as dry as a plate of chilli chicken (with bone) from Chung Wah Restaurant and Bar on Chowringhee in Kolkata. This is the case since Mohandas Gandhi ('Karamchand' will always be Pankaj

Kapoor in the 80s eponymous detective show) wrote down in his will that in exchange of bequeathing his face on all currency notes, independent India will not drink on his birthday. Being the uncontested bapu of a mai-baap state, his writ became the lo and behold.

But no matter, it wasn't as if we couldn't raise a glass to Lal Bahadur Shastri, the teetotaller prime minister who never had a problem about others drinking on his birthday which he shares with teetotalitarian Gandhi. It was just that we had to ensure that we didn't run out of the good stuff the evening before so as to raise that celebratory glass.

Pre-Gandhi Jayantis always resemble a New Year's Eve party where the next day's hangover is laying off the juice, at least at bars and restaurants. On 1 October, even Godse fanboys line up moderately patiently outside and inside thekas like scraggly human centipedes waiting to pull the cap off the bottle. In 2020, I was part of a disciplined queue keeping 'do gaz duri' in our individual mix of Caucasian, Dravidian and Mongolian chalk circles outside a liquor store during one dry day eve. But things quickly returned to normal, with the standard pushing and shoving the next dry day. By 2021, I was ordering Swiggy Genie on hot, humid, if not dry, days.

In their 1988 book, *Manufacturing Consent: The Political Economy of the Mass Media*, economist Edward S. Herman and linguist Noam Chomsky described manufacured consent as 'a system-supportive propaganda function, by reliance on market forces, internalized assumptions, and self-censorhip, and without overt coercion'. Dry days are manufactured consent to prohibition with covert, moralistic coercion. Only a brave person will raise a genuine toast to Mohandas Gandhi's seated statue outside Parliament on that happy day.

Dry days also witness a manufactured demand. A pent-up demand means, for most plonkers, an artificially created surge: 'Gotta go to the theka today to pick up stock, tomorrow's dry!' This is a real-world equivalent of the James DeMonaco 2013 dystopian horror film, *The Purge*. Mohandas Gandhi, for all his abhorrence of violence, would have appreciated the depiction of the villain in the movie—the rich—if not the treatment meted out to them. White picket-fenced suburban America, it turns out at least in the movies, is not quite Gram Swaraj.

The Purge is set in an alternate 2014, where the 'New Founding Fathers of America' are elected to power after an economic collapse that comes with its strain of social and law and order breakdown. It's a kind of 'If people cared two hoots about the 2G scam beyond wanting a change of curtains' situation. The Fathers of the Nation—the Bapus in wigs, if you will—bring order and establish the annual event of the Purge. In its own way, it's *one* Wet Day surrounded by 364 days of Dry Days. All crime, including murder, rape, arson, is legal for 12 hours, and emergency services like ambulances, hospitals, fire and police services are shut from 7pm on 21 March to 7am on 22 March every year.

Unlike in *The Purge*, a Dry Day doesn't have a siren to announce its start and end. Instead, we have signs either hastily written or neatly printed outside a liquor store stating the day and date the shop will be shut. For those who miss this sign and who do end up visiting a shut store on a dry day, a certain kind of sorrow, a sense of failing takes over. It is not only about having to do without alcohol when you want to do with alcohol that leaves your heart in a lurch. But it is also about being hit by your dereliction of duty—the duty of knowing dry days before they can disarm you and your loved ones.

You peer into the store if it's a private store with a glass front, or smell and feel the steel of the shutter with your face if it's a government liquor store, knowing that you have failed, that you were too late, and you need to get your shit together if you care to live the rest of your adult life responsibly. The darkness inside a liquor store is compelling proof that the world is a hostile, taunting place.

Save up for a rainy day: *Scene from Sharaabi, 1984, dir. Prakash Mehra*

So, why do we have so many dry days again? As I said, its purpose is to remind us not just that drinking is bad—not for health, but bad, in the sense that racism, casteism, making chomping sounds while eating is bad, and the way George Thorogood in his 1982 song, 'Bad to the Bone' says, 'B-A-A-A-D', as if a drunk goat has been found fumbling about outside Karim's in Old Delhi on an Eid night. Every time you knock back or slurp on a whisky or vodka, the dry day lurking will remind you that your knocking back and slurping is *wrong*.

Which is where we go back to the man with a strong 42.8% V/V sense of right and wrong, Mohandas Gandhi. He didn't like alcohol; he didn't like others to like alcohol; he wanted no one to have it. And it turns out that if we ignore him on this front, then we will be apparently insulting him in every other. Which to me is weird. I can understand people following him blindly as if on moonshine when he said, 'Go home, Simon!' But to imagine him saying, 'Simon says: Stop drinking' and then stopping? Really?

Gandhi, for all his PG Wodemousey Edwardianisms, was an eminent Victorian. Like abstinence on the sexual front, crossing one's legs to alcohol was something he found not just morally satisfying, but also aesthetically pleasing. If he had been a punk rock musician, he would have probably carried around a guitar with the words, 'Teetolarism: Beautiful as a bottle smashed against a drinker's face.' No, he was not.

And as a crypto-Protestant, he must have taken to the

temperance movement in Britain and the United States in his early manhood with gusto. I handled my early dislike of both the taste and effects of alcohol by accepting drinks and then surreptitiously, incrementally pouring the contents of my glass in my hosts' flower pots and/or kitchen sinks. Like liking Dylan, liking drinks either takes a bit of time, or it never happens at all. Like liking 'Gangnam Style', that infectious ditty by PSY, you become anti-alcohol instantly.

Gandhi was also famously under the influence of Leo Tolstoy. But the Russian writer, as we shall see, was less fundoo about drinking than his fanboy. To a Dr P.S. Alexeyef's 1890 book, *On Drunkenness*, Tolstoy had written the preface, wonderfully and insightfully titled, 'Why Do Men Stupefy Themselves?' It was less of an admonition and more of a genuine inquiry into why so many fellow Russians choose to get blotto.

> When observing his own life, a man may often notice in himself two different beings: the one is blind and physical, the other sees and is spiritual. The blind animal being eats, drinks, rests, sleeps, propagates, and moves, like a wound-up machine. The seeing, spiritual being that is bound up with the animal does nothing of itself, but only appraises the activity of the animal being; coinciding with it when approving its activity, and diverging from it when disapproving...

Tolstoy goes on to elucidate that the manifestation of the 'seeing, spiritual being' is what we call 'conscience'. And then he hits the proverbial bottle on the head:

> When a man is sober he is ashamed of what seems all right when he is drunk. In these words we have the essential underlying cause prompting men to resort to stupefiers. People resort to them either to escape feeling ashamed after having done something contrary to their consciences, or to bring themselves beforehand into a state in which they can commit actions contrary to conscience, but to which their animal nature prompts them.

That is a pretty *accurate* decription of why an overwhelmingly majority of drinkers drink: to feel less inhibited about doing things you'd think twice about when sober. Like fight in a war, or put an arm around a woman, or attempt to burn a £20 note because, as someone who finds the British royal family a pan without a flash, you don't like the face of the late monarch on the currency...This is a function that ethanol serves when blood alcohol levels reach medium to high, depending on body weight and moral convenience.

The beauty and the truth in Tolstoy's observation is revealing. He admits that when drinking does not stifle the conscience, thereby not leading to the committing of any wrongs or crimes, drinking is fine. Like his Indian admirer, he preferred people abstaining from alcohol. But unlike the former, he didn't mind temperance. Interestingly, while the Russian was an 'ardent believer' of sexual abstinence, he was not abhorred by others having sex, like Gandhi. It is to be noted, India does not have 'No Sex' Day on 2 October or any other date on the calendar.

> Alcohol or liquor include the country-made liquor and arak, besides the large quantity of liquor imported from foreign countries. All these should be strictly prohibited. Alcohol makes a man forget himself and while its effects last, he becomes utterly incapable of doing anything useful. Those who take a drinking, ruin themselves and ruin their people. They lose all sense of decency and propriety.
>
> There is a school who favour limited and regulated consumption of alcohol and believe it to be useful. I have not found any weight in their argument. Even if we accept their view for a moment, we have still to face the fact that innumerable human beings cannot be kept under discipline. Therefore, it becomes our duty to prohibit alcoholic drinks even if it were only for the sake of this vast majority.

Gandhi was a teetotalitarian. Thankfully for drinkers in this country, the great man had his hands busy with other more meaningful projects. It was not drinking per se, I assume, he found abhorrent but its effects, of inebriation, of bad behaviour like urinating on fellow passengers on a flight. He was, in all likelihood, petrified-disgusted of drunken behaviour as many of us, drinkers included, are. But for him drinking *was* drunkenness, a conflation that others less influenced by Victorian morals and etiquette were less inclined towards. For him, drinking and peeing on someone after getting drunk were pretty much the same action.

But this is not a trait of an arch conservative in matters

social—counterpointing this mindset with radical politics. Take the 19th-century mystic Gadadhar Chattopadhyay a.k.a. Ramakrishna Paramhansa, the man whose framed picture you're liable to find in every Bengali household prayer corner outside the plains of Kolkata's Ballygunge. There is one notable instance when Girish Chandra Ghosh, the doyen of Bengali theatre, and his disciple appeared at Ramakrishna's home tanked up. *Sri Sri Ramkrishnakathamrita* (The Gospel of Sri Ramkrishna) chronicled by Mahendra Nath Gupta, better known as 'Sri Mo', or the very Fritz Lang-meets-James Bond-sounding 'Mr M', records the meeting that took place on 1 September 1885:

> Girish Ghosh and two of his friends arrived in a carriage. He had drunk a bit. He entered sobbing and started crying at Thakur's [Ramakrishna's] feet.
>
> Ramkrishna lovingly started patting his body. He called out to one of his disciples: 'Oi, get him some tobacco.'

Ghosh, according to M, blabbers on about Ramakrishna being the Real McCoy ('purnobrahma'), adding that if that's not true, everything is false. (Personally, I use the phrase 'Mrityu anivarja', or death is inevitable, to signal to both myself and anyone else in the vicinity that I'm Hemingway drunk, considering by being Rimbaud drunk I will not remember anything the next day.) The great doyen of Bengali theatre goes on to plead that he takes care of Ramakrishna for a year. The older man tut-tuts him, telling the drunk man, 'The people here aren't good—they'll talk,' and politely refuses the invitation. The sentimental sot then goes on to try to cure Ramakrishna—who by then was suffering from throat cancer, which would kill him less than a year later at 50—by blowing on his throat.

By now, a bit irritated by Ghosh's behaviour, M tells us that Ramakrishna was saved not so much by the bell, but the coachman calling him. He had come up to fetch his passenger. And here M, Boswell to Ramakrishna's Johnson, notes that the concerned Ramakrishna, Sherlock to M's Watson tells his diarist, 'Go with him, check where he goes—hope he doesn't hit him [the coachman].'

The concern is charming. Ramakrishna seems equally concerned about the tipsy Ghosh and the coachman working overtime. Without knowing—'And what is knowing?' as Ramakrishna must have said—we have taken to this approach to drink and the usual drunk: a mix of bemusement and concern, not always for the same person.

As Indian passport-holders coming under the Indian Penal Code, no matter where we stand on identifying ourselves as citizens, we must thank our fellow countrymen that in deference to the Great Gandhi's wishes, we don't have dry days every day. The list of dry days is long, all of them barring one having nothing to do with Gandhi's 'birthday wishes'. But can I be frank with you? Every day the liquor stores are shut, it only doubles the keenness for the glug.

It leaves us Gandhi happy. As is Khopdi, one of my all-time heroes and antidotes for all kinds of fundamentalists, the resident drunk in Kundan Shah and Saeed Mirza's delightful 1986 television series, Nukkad (Street Corner). Khopdi played by the great Sameer Khakhar, passed away—not just passed out anymore—in March 2023, has left our neighbourhoods dry.

Raising a patiala to dry days. Après ceux-là, le déluge!

ROTI RISING

Conflicts of economic interests grew more acute with the increasing nearness of Europe; Indian industries, and particularly the ancient cotton industry, suffered from legislation that favoured the British manufacturer. A piece of incredible folly on the part of the company precipitated an outbreak.

—*The Outline of History* (1920), H.G. Wells

Whenever I hear the word 'postcolonial', I reach for my imaginary stick of cotton candy. It's soft, weightless yet changes form the moment it touches my tongue becoming less magical and suddenly with more weight than it set out to be. It's also sugary, bordering on an endless chew of kitsch-clichés. And yet, it is dazzlingly voluminous and Commonwealth pink.

But for me, 'colonisation' and 'colony', yet to be bent into 'colonial' and still far removed from 'postcolonial', conjure up a different set of images and notions: Mars, the Moon, the seventh planet around the F-type star Kepler-90 in the constellation Draco some 2,790 light years away from us. Blame it on a diet of Campa Cola and science fiction books—especially the AE van Vogt novels lent to me by the nonagenarian Jesuit ex-mathematics teacher Father Goreaux in school—colonisation for me meant setting up a human colony in uninhabited planets and spots of outer and deeper space. It didn't involve meeting indigenous populations on these planets, ruffling their feathers, taking over their planet, or ruling their societies. Those were subjects for the 'alien invasion' kind of science fiction of which HG Wells' 1897 *The War of the Worlds* was an early example.

Colonisation or space exploratory SF, of course, was just one kind in which humans—brave, challenged, curious, and largely benign—journey forth to either find new homes or survive. Andy Weir's novels, *The Martian* and *Artemis*, for instance, are Robinson Crusoe-style survivor and Louis Lamour-kind Wild Lunar settlement stories, respectively. But quickly enough, I caught on to how humans were rarely presented as the alien invaders in the strictest of terms. Yes, people from a planet(s) invaded other people on a planet, but these were mostly still intra-species conflicts—like wars in 18th-century Europe. As far as inter-species inter-planetary invasions went, the aliens were always the space invaders, never humans.

The history books, it turns out, didn't have things going so one-way. I only realised that 'colonial' was tied at the hip to 'colony' when it also struck me that while a colony on Mars was a Martian colony, one on the Moon was a lunar colony, India was once a *British* colony, even if going by the same rules of nomenclature, it should have been called an Indian colony. One contradiction led to new confusions, and suddenly I found myself in a postcolonial age where in the books and movies, 'Earth' populated by mostly White people were all the time invaded by aliens, never the other way around. For any exploratory mission from Earth, the Prime Directive, as established by Star Trek's Star Fleet—a prohibition on interference with other cultures and civilisations so as to not come in the way of their 'normal development'—of course, applies.

Which is when it struck me that White humans had indeed been aliens, long enough for many of us in India to believe that we are, and speak 'Klingon'. This revelation—not quite '666' in the deluge of colonial history that has been and continues to be vaped in public and academic discourse—led me to the following alien invasion story. Mind you, it is an alien invasion story, not an exploratory, colonising, or colonial one.

***

The first reports of the arrival of the Outworlders had started to come in almost a month ago. They didn't come in dribs and trickles, but in one flow, with new information layered on top of old ones in qayedas, peshkars, relas, mukhras and mohras. As Miyan Basant covered both tops of his tabla with a freshly washed pair of cloth, wedging in the small hammer in between two hoops and against a dowel of the

Close encounters of the nineteenth-century kind:
Generative AI, cfhdesign

baya, and pushing both pieces under the bed, he looked up once outside the door into the courtyard. He was aiming for the evening sky, but he caught Noor sitting in front of the oven flipping a roti instead.

There had been rumours of sightings near Ajrara. Long hawaiships, wide enough to cast longer shadows on the ground below in the autumn sun. Reports of their numbers were imprecise. Some were saying that half a dozen had passed Bhagwanpur, Nalpur, Mundali and Chak Morna over the last week. There were even reports that a flotilla of about fifty had docked in Delhi. Two of Miyan's young students, the brothers Kallu and Miru Khan, insisted that their uncle had actually seen some of the Outworlders in the Moree Gate area. Others like Ghanshyam, who had returned from the capital last week after making his usual weekly sorties and trade, insisted that the Outlanders, flour-white inside their scarlet armour and black helmets, hardly ventured out of their ships during the day. Only some were spotted at night not far from their massive transportations.

The hot rotis piling up in the yet-to-be-tied-up bundle next to Noor glistened in the moonlight. Before each one joined the stack, they went through a singular procedure. The flattened circle of dough would lie on the hot, stone tawa, waiting, while Noor turned it with her slim fingers. Then they would simmer and, as if to command, rise like a lung, like a breathing tabla surface, until it collapsed back into flatness as soon as Noor flung it into the pile.

Miyan smiled to himself as he imagined the roasted black spots on each circle of bread resembling the black circles of the syahis on tabla tops. The syahis were also made of flour and water, and the musician liked the comparison he had just made in his head. He stepped out, and closer in the light of the now dimming flames noticed the unleavened frown on Noor's forehead.

'I think we should be staying at my brother's for a few weeks,' she said, dealing out a couple of rotis like cards onto Miyan's plate already wet with a pool of daal and sabzi on the side. 'Phulera's and Shamshed Tyagi's families have already moved. These are not rumours any more.'

'Yes, I heard,' Miyan said in between chewing. 'But going to Lucknow in these circumstances is hardly helpful. It's better to be here. What can happen in a village like this?'

Noor was about to say something, but kept quiet, instead

bringing the water pitcher closer. Her husband was not taking the threat of the hawaiships hovering so close to Ajrara seriously. His answer to all problems and threats was his tabla classes. There were times when she really felt like stabbing the skins of those tablas with her kitchen knife, no matter what the consequences. True, he was a good man, caring even. But in the face of any kind of danger, Miyan Basant just turned the other way, waiting for the storm to blow over, or even, through him. Two years ago, it had seemed as if Miyan and Noor were the only household who'd stayed put when the Kali Nadi broke its banks and gulped everything down its maw. Not just in Ajrara, but in neighbouring Badoli, Atuala and Mundali. Certainly, Miyan's jowar crop had been destroyed, and with no farm hands available till winter, the two of them seemed destined to suffer and then be snuffed out altogether.

So much for all the talk of progress that still came wafting from Lucknow and Delhi. Here in Ajrara, all that was modern and gleaming seemed to only reside in Miyan Basant's three pairs of tablas. But the threat of the Otherworlders was real. Even though this time around, no one had left the village, everyone was consciously and unconsciously looking up at the day and night skies. Especially at the night skies, the real black waters. It was no coincidence that these days, Ajrara's residents thought of their Kali Nadi and kaala paani—the very thought of crossing the black waters to an alien land—in the same thought tabla roll.

***

By the middle of winter, Meerut had become one of the many Outworlder outposts. Their domination had been swift, expansive and unnerving for people. Ajrara was not overlooked. The Thakurdwara Temple had been converted into a garrison for the aliens. It was still unclear whether they were an outright hostile force or not. Some of them were visible even during the day, having made encounters with locals that included Rahim Khan and Ustad Pehlai, and other village grandees. But the Outworlders made it be understood that no large gathering would be allowed. And that they were to replace Lucknow and Delhi rule.

A round man with frog eyes and a constant veneer of sweat even in winter was their intermediary. It was soon found that his name was Ram Dewal, a resident of Delhi and a teacher by trade. He translated the information and decrees that the Outworlders needed to communicate to the locals. 'He looks like a pig,' Kallu Khan had exclaimed before being shushed by his teacher. Miyan would not have all this gup-shup during tabla lessons, even though he did mark the fact that Noor, too, had made similar observations regarding the Dilliwala in the employment of the Outworlders.

But Miyan's escape through tabla—through the alleys and lanes and bylanes of its taali, khaali and soom, the play on the kinaras of its peripheries and on the syahis of its centres, and the palm, thumb, fingers and wrists of his students—had clearly been disrupted. His distaste for the flashy show of the Lucknow and Delhi schools of tabla-playing grew over the weeks. The very Dhit Dhits, Dhagetitas,

Dhir Dhirs, Gadigins that he had found abhorrent—'These gharanas encourage only the show-off! Mindless showing off!'—he had screamed more than once to more than one of his students.

The presence of those flour-white, red-clothed beings, with strange striations like gills down their chins, and carrying deadly fire-emitting pikes, along with the constant hum of their docked ships and their guttural, donkey hooves-click tongue, made his style of tabla-playing and tabla-teaching, for which families from as far as Meerut town would send their boys to him, suffer.

And then, at that turn where the coldness of northern winter steps into the coolness of early spring, matters became apparent. Mughis Ahmad, the man with one of the largest sugarcane farms in the region, had been a bulwark of society. Through his ministrations and largesse, Ajrara had not only become famous for its music, but over the decades, with technological methods imported from the enterprising Scindias, it had also become one of the largest revenue generators of the Yamuna doab.

'There will be no majlis this year, Miyan-saab. The Lal Kurtis have stopped it.' Chattar Lal had confirmed while visiting the tabla school to pay the month's fees for his rather talented son, Chaman. Miyan had been agitated for a while now. Usually, by this time, an invitation from Mughis Ahmad's estate to attend and perform at the annual music majlis was a given. Noor and he had even commented on whether Mamman Khan, the rising star from Wajid Ali

Shah's court in Lucknow, would return this year. There had been some talk about the Lucknow boy having fallen out of favour with the Awadh court.

'The Lal Kurtis had apparently told Mughis and other zamindars that spending money on any majlis or festival is a colossal waste. This, after they had already diverted pretty much all of this season's sugarcane crop to their own hawaiships. Last Friday, their men found Mughis holding out a large stockpile behind the mandi at Kharkhoda.'

'And?'

'And Mughis was dragged out from his zenana, in broad moonlight, and they've taken over his estate. They have, according to Sahansar Pal, not just defiled the kitchens there, but have taken to confiscating sugarcane harvests from other smaller growers too.'

Miyan Basant had no doubt now that the Lal Kurtis—the name by which the Otherworlders were known by now because of their red armour made out of a thick fabric—were indeed a hostile force. Over the next few months, Ajrara was festering with the smell of slaughtered nilgai and wild boars. They clearly did not find the vermin to be unpalatable. But over and above this noxious smell of flesh and hair hung the sickly sweet smell of crushed sugarcane from the Otherworlder hawaiships.

'They only eat meat,' Noor had said, her nose crinkling up as if the mutton she had served had, by some alchemic putrefaction, turned into wild boar meat. 'They may not have anything else in their diet. But what I don't understand is why they have to make such an open, obnoxious display of what they eat.'

Miyan ate quietly. With no majlis and only a handful of students coming, his mood had turned fast and hard. He was a man who rarely felt anger, anger in his book being a disruption, something that the Lucknow baaj louts were adept at as they went berserk with their open strokes on the lau of the tabla between the central syahi and kinar on the edges. The thought of the Lal Kurtis one day developing a gharana of their own repelled and fascinated him at the same time. To stop himself from pursuing such a line of thought especially while having dinner, he tore his last roti in half, wiped off the mutton gravy with it and stuffed it in his mouth whole.

'Ustad Miyan Basant?' The voice crept up behind both Noor and him. Turning around quickly he saw the ghee-shine of Ram Dewal's face. But it was the longish, deadwhite face behind, that glowed both in the remnants of the oven flame and moonlight, which made Miyan reply.

'Yes, I am Miyan.' Noor shuffled her way with the empty utensils inside, leaving the leftovers to be gathered later. She also caught the faces of both visitors, especially that of the chalkwhite one, who was making no attempts to keep his fire-pike out of view.

Turning his pallid face towards Miyan, the Outworlder then spoke directly. A gentle breeze was blowing. But Miyan doubted whether the flutter of the Lal Kurti's gash-like gills had anything to do with it. It was the usual clicks and palate sounds that came out of the alien's mouth. In his thick-tongued Dilli Hindustani, Ram Dewal followed, 'Sirjan Pathrik Maqdaf here says that you are one of only three people in Ajrara who have land that does not cultivate sugarcane. Why is that?'

Miyan looked at the translator. His thick lips and Delhi drawl made him almost as unintelligible as the taller figure next to him. But Miyan knew that the longer he'd delay a reply, the longer these two would linger. With his eyes now set on Sirjan Pathrik Maqdaf, Miyan explained, 'I teach the tabla. That is my job, my craft. I am not a farmer. On the small land that I own here, I grow some jowar, nothing fancy. It requires little attention, certainly far less water than cane, and it survives droughts that I can tell you sugarcane crops have not in the past. I also don't keep more than two farmhands. We use the jowar for our own use. Any remainder—which is very little anyway—is sold to Mughis Ahmad. I am not in the practice of wasting.'

At the mention of Mughis Ahmad, Sirjan Pathrik stiffened, not unlike a yellow stalk of cane. At the courtyard where all three stood, only the light of the lamp pushed out some of the evening darkness. But the Lal Kurti's pale, almost grey, eyes could probably see through the dark. He said something in a low voice to Ram Dewal. 'Is that made from your crop?' the Dilliwala asked Miyan, pointing at the pile of rotis next to the lamplight.

'Yes, jowar roti,' Miyan replied in a plain voice ready to change its pitch. He thought he heard Noor's bangles clink against one other, but he may have been mistaken.

The white figure stepped forward, picked up a roti lying on top of the untied cloth. He looked at it once as if inspecting an ornament or instrument, and then, pushing his pike back against his shoulder, rolled the roti into a handkerchief and took a bite off its top. It was an act of aggression, but also of curious exploration. The three figures stood there, as the Lal Kurti chewed. After what seemed like minutes, he looked once at Miyan, not menacingly, but with suspicion, then once at the house next to which they were standing, dark except for a dim flicker of a light inside one of the rooms.

The white figure said something after another chomp. Ram Dewal translated, 'So no sugar in this?'

'You know very well, Dulalji, this is roti. How on earth will it have sugar in it?'

The Dilliwala said nothing. Just gave a brisk shake of his head to the Lal Kurti. Just as they had arrived out of nowhere, the two of them left, without fuss, without any signal. As Miyan picked up the bundle of rotis and leftovers and went inside before bolstering the door, he realised that the Lal Kurti by the name of Sirjan Pathrik Maqdaf had left clutching the half-eaten roti in his left hand like a rag. He shook his head.

Later that night in bed, he would simply mention, 'What is the world coming to?' Noor would sigh in return, hoping that her husband would dream one of his happy tabla dreams. The ones which made his fingers move even in his sleep and would make her happy.

***

The death of Sgt Patrick McDuff was not immediately seen as a matter of concern by the occupying Boadicean forces. New terrains came with new hazards, both in terms of bio-planetary conditions as well as native challenges that were described in records as political. But by the next year, fatalities had mounted to a point of no return. The swiftness and savagery with which personnel died, in many cases literally standing, was astounding.

Those afflicted by the scourge had shown the same signs—skin turning hard and brittle almost overnight; then the whole body covered with a powdery incrustation, that was accompanied by the total collapse of the respiratory system. The ships' doctors had initially suspected that it was a variant of what the locals called kala-azar, or black fever. But after much consultation, the epidemic was found to be something else, with its source in the Doab region, its epicentre at the village of Ajrara in the tehsil of Meerut.

In their report, Boadicean virologists unanimously found the outbreak specifically affecting the colonists, leaving natives unaffected. Soon enough, the culprit was found to be C_4 carbon fixation, and toxic levels of malic acid formation left in the bodies. Either through ingestion or via contact, the Boadicean respiratory system—otherwise perfectly suitable in the conditions of the Jagat 3 hydrocarbon-based ecosystem—was severely compromised. But with no antidote found, the decision to abandon the planet was finally taken.

Out of the forty-five colonies across the planet, thirty-one were devastated by the time Jagat 3 was abandoned. The mission—so successful otherwise in finding rich sucrose deposits so valuable for sucrose-depleted Boadicean energy requirements and inter-planetary trade, and to power their $C_{12}H_{22}O_{11}$ hydrogen-stripping plasma engines on their ships—was shut down. The appearance of jowar rotis across Boadicean outposts, in front of barrack entrances, constabularies, missions and even ships only worsened matters.

In the early onslaught of the outbreak, the Boadicean magistrate of Mathura had recorded in his speakdoc: 'One day as I entered the office I found four little cakes laid on the table, dirty little cakes of the coarsest flour, about the size and thickness of a biscuit. A man had come to a village, and given a cake to the watchman, with injunctions to bake four like it, to distribute them to the watchmen of the adjacent villages, and desire them to do the same. The watchmen obeyed, but at the same time informed the police they had now reported the affair, sending in the cakes. The following day came similar reports from other parts of the district, and we next learnt that these cakes were being distributed in the same manner over all of Upper India.'

'Upper India', as the Boadiceans had named the expansive and blurred region under the Saiyads, Jats and Gujjars, may have been where the mysterious distribution of 'cakes' had started, but this practice had spread quickly across the sucrose-producing parts of Jagat 3. The Boadiceans destroyed these dough cakes–rotis—and very soon outlawed their production across the planet, making cane and paddy the mandatory crop. But if you cannot find the outlaw, whom can you punish to set an example?

Miyan and Noor were among the thousands across the world who saw the hawaiships blaze their engines and leave, feeling their shuddering engines and shimmering blue flamelights in their wake. Like the Lal Kurti epidemic that had been 'in the air,' the Lal Kurti occupational forces themselves took on the powdery edge of a legend, and then like a mist, of a rumour.

Miyan Basant was annoyed when he heard that Miru and Kallu Khan had decided to pursue their tabla in, of all places, Delhi.

'Sitab Khan saab has agreed to take us on as students,' Miru told him, barely hiding his excitement while his brother looked nervously everywhere but in Miyan's direction. Miyan had heard Sitab at Mughis Ahmad's annuals one year. What he had said then, seated somewhere in the middle of that large hall, still applied to Sitab Khan and the Delhi gharana as a whole: 'Bloody pakhawaj players pretending to be tabla masters!'

But never mind, he told himself now crossing his legs and settling down for dinner. Youngsters today were all agog with the loud, flashy structures of peshkars and qayedas. These lot could go to the dogs with the Lal Kurtis, whose departure seemed to have brought about a new, restless excitement among the young. A new gharana, Miyan groaned inside, would as surely follow. Noor placed another hot roti on Miyan's plate, making his visible grumble subside.

'Achha, Noor, why do they call rotis chapatis in Delhi? Aren't they the same thing?' he said, tearing a piece and dipping it into a fresh bowl of daal.

'I don't exactly know. But from what Amina and some others who lived in Delhi before coming here after getting married say, chapati is simply roti that rises in the heat of the oven flame. Chapati is the name for fluffy roti.'

'But when it cools and subsides, the chapati becomes roti again?'

'I guess,' Noor said with a smile.

Miyan Basant gave out a rare, unleavened laugh. He was going to have another roti made of the jowar off his own land that bore no sugarcane.

WHAT DO YOU KNOW OF MY FOOTBALL WHO ONLY FOOTBALL KNOW?

I get asked a lot, including by my sniggering self, 'How come you're so much into following a game that no team in India can play?' This is an attempt to answer that quite valid question.

First of all, at the cost of putting words in people's mouths including my own, the real question is why do I invest so much in the successes and failures of two footballing sides that I have no other connection with, barring the game, and in the successes and failures of another footballing side I may have connections with but whose quality of play, especially when compared to the first two sides, are, well, abysmal.

Since a while now, I have tied my own sense of worth to three footballing entities more than to any other non-personal thing: Argentina, Arsenal and Mohun Bagan. In no particular order of importance, the fortunes of these three mean more to me than the state of the country, state, city, school and college I once went to, public figures I admire, cultural landmarks, political parties I vote for, and all such things. The disparity between the three chosen barometers of my happiness and sadness are obvious: Argentina is a national side, Arsenal an English football club, and Mohun Bagan an Indian one.

When friends ask me which team I would support on a given day if two of the three play against each other, my reply is as logical as it is swift: the chances of Argentina playing either Arsenal or Mohun Bagan are nil, the first being a national side, the other two being clubs. As for Arsenal playing against Bagan, being on two separate continents and playing in leagues and tournaments whose Venn diagram circles are very unlikely to overlap—unless it's an exhibition match like the New York Cosmos with Pelé playing Mohun Bagan in 1977 (final scoreline: 2-2)—thereby not forcing me to choose between the angel and the shallow inviting sea.

Perhaps, it's best to simply say how I fell in love—there is no other expression to describe it—with the three.

The first time I came across a variation of CLR James's famous line, 'What do they know of cricket who only cricket know?' was in an op-ed article in a Kolkata (then still going by the official name of Calcutta at least in English) newspaper. It was, as is typical of op-ed writers in Kolkata dailies to this day, not about James or cricket, but something else that I don't remember. But as fate would have it, the author of the article had kindly mentioned the source of the line he had tweaked, which led me to find out James's origin in his 1963 book, *Beyond a Boundary*, itself a tweak of the line from Rudyard Kipling's 1891 poem, 'The English Flag': 'What do they know of England who only England know?'

It took me a while to understand the meaning of this rondeau. Then it took at least a few years—confirmations coming in long gaps from other sources—to confirm that what I'd understood as the meaning of that line was indeed what its writer intended. From where I stand now, I believe the point being repeatedly made in the construct by Kipling and made cool by CLR James is that to understand West Indian cricket/England/Dilwale Dulhania Le Jayenge/kulfi-faluda, [choose your phenomenon], you need to know its social and cultural context(s).

So, what do you know of *my* football who only football know? Let me count the ways:

Mohun Bagan AC
Year of Fealty: 1977

At an age when loving football meant playing it, Mohun Bagan appeared as an entity that showed me the way the way Obi-Wan showed young Skywalker. My extended family was unequivocally and vocally Bagan supporters. Not much discussion, dialogue or argument went into it. While my father's family voted CPI(M) and my mother's Congress, there was no question—none was ever raised—of supporting any other club than Mohun Bagan.

This was the 1970s-early 1980s, a time when Kolkata

footballing lines were still drawn along 'legacy' and 'origin' parameters: Mohun Bagan if one was 'ghoti' (roots in western pre-Partition Bengal), East Bengal if one was 'bangaal' (roots in eastern pre-Partition Bengal and pre-1971 East Pakistan). Mohammedan Sporting if you were Muslim. There were exceptions, but they were rare, and usually had explanations in personal history such as a son rejecting his father's club because of semi-Oedipal reasons; because of some favourite senior in school or dada in the neighbourhood who drew one out to the 'Dark Side'.

(You could also support a local side that was not one of the Big Three. But usually that was always an add-on, the way being a Rajasthan Royal supporter in IPL cricket is an add-on for an India supporter. And no one really took being, say, a Calcutta Port Trust supporter seriously.)

There was a certain swag, even comfort, in maintaining and propagating these quietly foisted clan lines. Growing up, I would follow the exploits of my favourite Bagan players and teams. 'Follow' then meant reading about them in the two magazines I would get at home: *Khela* (Play/Sports) and the sports section of *Anandamela*. A bit later, these were joined by the sports pages of Bengali and English newspapers. There was also the occult practice of cutting out photos of players and pasting them in my scrapbook as if it was my future wedding album.

And there was the supremely exotic figure of Roy Race. 'Rovers-er Roy,' the Bengali translation of the British comic strip, Roy of the Rovers, was a regular page in one of the two fortnightly children's magazines, *Anandamela*, I used to devour. (I still pick up occasional issues, and its Durga Puja annual without fail, whether I read their contents or not.) Even in the initial black and white frames of the strip that first appeared in 1954 as a weekly feature in the British comic magazine, *Tiger*, it was obvious that Roy was a blond, English footballer playing for a club called the Melchester Rovers.

The sheer genius of the creation by writer Frank S. Pepper and artist Joe Colquhoun lay in merging the possible (hi-jinks football action) with the fantastical (shots into goals and passes from impossible angles, runs that were not allowed by the laws of physics—until quantum football was unlocked on 22 June 1986 at Mexico's Azteca Stadium). The same sport which Rovers-er Roy made me wait patiently for in the next issue of *Anandamela* was actually the football being played in 1970s–1980s Kolkata grounds. But not quite.

If you search for Bidesh Bose on Google, the first entry the search engine will throw up will be the Wikipedia entry of 'Bidesh Ranjan Bose'. It introduces him as 'a former Indian Bengali international footballer and politician from West Bengal'. The only other line pertaining to any footballing past reads: 'As a player, he appeared with Mohun Bagan AC in club football.' It goes on to say how he won the 'Uluberia Purba constituency seat in 2021 West Bengal assembly election as candidate of All India Trinamool Congress' and that he was awarded the Banga Bhushan title by the West Bengal government in 2014. That's like describing

Hark! The herald angles sing! *From 'Rovers-er Roy', Bengali translation of 'Roy of the Rovers', writer Frank S Pepper, artist Joe Colquhoun, Anandamela, March 1981*

Muhammad Ali as 'a professional American boxer who was the subject of Johnny Wakelin and the Kinshasha Band's 1974 hit, "Black Superman"'!

Bidesh, in his green and maroon Mohun Bagan jersey, staring toothfully out of a magazine, was my man. As was the great Shyam Thapa; I was too young to watch his legendary bicycle kick goal against eternal rivals East Bengal at the 1978 Calcutta Football League final, but have read dozens of written descriptions where any exaggeration is underrated. Such as Moti Nandy's description in the 6 August 1978 edition of *Anandabazar Patrika* that must, by law, be quoted at length:

> Subhash [Bhoumik] is swaying as he moves up the right flank with the ball along with Satyajit [Mitra]. Right or left, Satyajit isn't able to read which way Subhash will move forward. He leans forward once to the right, once to the left and that's where he loses a fraction of a second to Subhash. Subhash takes the ball to the goal line as required, sends the ball towards the goal. When the ball is going on its head-level precision trajectory, Manoranjan [Bhattacharya] stretches his forehead out in the path of the ball. The ball doesn't make proper contact with his forehead. It barely touches, but slightly changes its direction. And that is what brings disaster to East Bengal.
>
> That ball reaches the head of the predatory [Mohammed] Habib who has moved forward. Habib heads the ball ahead to the waiting Shyam [Thapa] with his back to

the goal. The ball is floating gently above the head and behind him is the goal. Now what? Should he trap the ball, turn his body and take a shot towards the goal? That will waste two seconds. Football by nature is about using time and space. Then?

A moment's thought and accordingly action. The way an ocean wave coils and foams with the pull of the tide and the crest of the wave sparkles with a diamond shine, a maroon-green wave was seen to expand with its face towards the sky and above it whipped out a leg.

***

Argentina National Team
Year of Fealty: 1986

The first time I registered a World Cup game was in 1982 when my parents were at their friends' house and a tiny, portable black and white TV was beaming a match live from Spain to Whakatane, a small town on the northern coastline of New Zealand (made famous by the eruption on 9 December 2019 of Whakaari/White Island off Whakatane's coast killing 22 people who were visiting the active volcano as part of a guided tour), where we lived then. On the kitchen counter, the screen showed football and so I started to watch.

Memories of much of what I witnessed that day, and once back home on our proper colour television in the days that followed, have been irreparably contaminated with what I have seen subsequently of the 1982 World Cup on television, even on big screen and, of course, on YouTube. But I do remember the Apollonian Zico scoring the first two goals in a group match against New Zealand, the bearded Socrates (I had never seen a bearded footballer before) leaning 45 degrees to stitch passes and dodge defenders, and these footballers in yellow and blue making needlework of a football field. I was, of course, supporting New Zealand, as everyone in school was. And yet, the 4-0 defeat left me confused about something else: if this is also football, it was football of another kind. The Portuguese words 'Jogo bonito'—Beautiful Game—were still unknown to me then. But it was only a matter of time before I knew what it was called in 'footballing circles'.

Armed with this televised knowledge, when I returned to India, I did not replace my (new) Bagan heroes with the newly acquired international stars. But they did start appearing more and more in my scrapbooks, their names being increasingly conjured when I played in my horseshoe lane becoming Zico, Rossi and Karl-Heinz Rummenigge—the favourite name I would like to mutter while I broke through the flanks, and was broken down before I could do any damage—along with the usual Bidesh, Mihir, Xavier, Manas, Shyam...

In 1982, I was 11; in 1986, I was 15, the four years marking a distance and time not fully comprehended by adults. Even as the footballers in the firmament both at home and away were pretty much all the same, by 1986, I was, with only cricket as a distraction, much more well-versed with the incantatory and celebratory aspects of football. I was primed, in hindsight, to be loyal not just to a football club, Mohun Bagan, but also to football itself. But everything went for a toss in the 1986 World Cup.

There is not much point in describing what millions of young and not-so-young people felt when they we were witness to Diego Maradona leading the Argentina squad. It was coup de foudre from Game 1 against South Korea. If there was a whole flotilla of reasons for me giving my heart to Bagan, there was only one why I tied my cart to the Argentina bull from the summer of 1986: Maradona.

Every World Cup—not to mention Copa Americas—it is the Albicelestes that have controlled my moods, my days, my appetite. When Argentina lost their opening game in the 2022 World Cup to Saudi Arabia, my heart felt like it had been sacrificed to Quetzalcoatl for some sin *I* had to atone for. When I pinned my hopes on sides not just with Maradona in them, but also with Claudio Caniggia, Gabriel Batistuta, Juan Román Riquelme, Lionel Messi since 1990 till 2018, why was my anguish personal, as if they were *my* chaps who had failed? I spoke neither their language, nor knew much about their culture, and yet, via this Arc de Triomphe I had entered in 1986, I was for all purposes Argentine for at least a few weeks every four years.

Which is why when the longue durée of desolation was lifted in Qatar—ending 32 years of disappointment—it felt not so much a great validation of a great footballing side, but the lifting of a curse. Loving Argentina, in any case, was always a Mephistophelian deal.

Over time, I have also realised why I chose Argentina;true, an Argentina introduced to me and encapsulated by that raging bull of demonic skill, hubris and no-matter-what-it-takes gangster chutzpah, but also an Argentina that created such a force, attempting—no matter the failings—to create more. In his 2016 book, *Angels with Dirty Faces: The Footballing History of Argentina*, Jonathan Wilson, goes to the source of what drew me to Argentina in the first place without knowing it:

> No country so intellectualises its football, so loves its theories and its myths. Football in Argentina is overtly cultural, overtly political. Presidents know its power and seek to harness it; the unscrupulous mobilise hooligan groups, the barras bravas, in their support. The philosophers meanwhile dismiss titles, whole generations of success, because they were won in the 'wrong way'.

What I had witnessed for the first time on a TV screen in the squelching heat of a 1986 Kolkata summer was not just Diego Maradona and his bandidos, but the furnace in which they and 'Argentina football' were smelted. That football, as seen on the field during games was just the tip of the iceberg of football, for better or worse, has been made most evident to me by Argentina. The qualities they hold, never mind of the School of Menotti (idealism) or of the School of Bilardo (pragmatism), are attractive to me. It's not just about the beauty of the game, but something more primal, more deep than skin and therefore, perhaps, less honest.

My Mephistopheles: *Maradona surging, 22 June 1986, Azteca Stadium, Mexico City, Getty*

My support to Argentina is like supporting the Kauravs. No matter the final scorelines after each Kurukshetra.

***

Arsenal
Year of Fealty: 1999

It was yet another 'accident' that brought me to the door of Highbury, north London home to Arsenal, a club I had followed as much and as little as any other English club as an international football-following tyke from the outer rim of 1980s Kolkata. (Incidentally, not once did 'Roy of the Rovers' of Melchester get me interested in either of the real 'Melchesters'. Manchester United I got to know from learning about the Munich air disaster in which eight

Manchester United players died, which in turn I found out after listening to The Beatles' 'Dig It' from their 1970 album *Let It Be*, where the name Matt Busby, legendary manager of Manchester United was roll-called along with that of Doris Day, BB King and the CIA.)

The accident was again in a World Cup, as late as the 1998 tournament in France, the first post-Maradona one where I followed Diego Simeone, Juan Sebastian Veron, Batistuta and Co. till the bitter end of the quarter final game against the Netherlands where a stoppage time Dennis Bergkamp goal ended the Argentina silver trail.

I knew Bergkamp played for Arsenal and was electric there. But it wasn't the flying Dutchman who inducted me into Goonerhood. It was a Frenchman—outshone by Zinedine Zidane, Patrick Viera and David Trezeguet—and yet who blew me away the way invisible sonic booms do and one is left staring at the empty sky. Thierry Henry appeared in my Poltergeist-friendly landlord's television set's screen as *the* phantom of the World Cup opera. I remember telling anyone who was around during the France matches that this player was divine and I would follow him wherever he goes.

Henry was, in 1998, playing for Monaco. In those days, I barely/did not have cable, so never mind Ligue 1, even Premier League games were unavailable to me. By 1999, I got to know that after a toe-dip in Juventus, he joined Arsenal, the Arsenal of 1999 Arsene Wenger, his old manager in Monaco. That first season in Arsenal—26 goals in a club that came second to Manchester United—was a sign of things to come.

And then I find, of course, Bergkamp already there. But this was not just about the club playing fabulous 'French-style' football, or the unbeaten Premier League run of 49 games from 2003 to 2004 earning them the title 'The Invincibles'. How would I have known all that in 1999 when I followed the glorious Henry into the Gooner Squad?

With all the ups and downs of the club since then, for me they always have a dependable quality, a workmanlike appeal that can break into Mary Poppins-Dick Van Dyke chimneysweepers' song'n'dance joie de vivre when things are joyous, and embarrassing like a drunken uncle stupor when they aren't. Arsenal, strange as it may sound for someone who got on to their red and white bus only around the turn of this century, is family.

***

So, here's the thing. My love for Mohun Bagan, Argentina and Arsenal, the triple goalposts through which I take my football kicks and love for the game personally, are made of a strange gestalt—the whole certainly greater than the parts, which include beauty, a regularly lubricated dislike of 'archrivals', irrational clanship, imagined community belonging, individuals bordering on the divine, swag, managers, tragedies, hauteur...

For someone who is constantly impressed by others rattling off facts and stats, recollecting footnotes in the history of the game, making devilishly clever breakdowns of devilishly clever match strategies—the hardcore—it would be quite dishonest for me to say my love of football and the holy trinity is based on what any serious follower/supporter would consider following/supporting.

My appreciation, loyalty, understanding, whatever you call it, is amplitude- and serotonin-based. My love for M-A-A rides on a constantly sine-curving mixture of shouting at the screen, crunching into the sofa, going into the dark, wishing hard bad thoughts, believing suddenly in a god...

And through this triptych I seek and find love in football.

THIS MAN'S PLACE IS NOT IN THE KITCHEN

The kitchen, for me, remains a sinkhole—a dark, dank, depressing place where like the Westerner's vision of Pakistani kids stitching top class footballs, women prepare food in one unending cycle only interrupted by life and other details. Of course, that's not what many kitchens we are familiar with are. The nice ones are 'modular', like some engineering project, but with softer edges, lighter hues, and stronger smells. And most are what can be assigned broadly as 'modern', at best pleasant, familiar spaces; at worst, practical slabs, cupboards, drawers and appliances that along with the bathroom is the room that needs a constant supply of water.

As you may have surmised, I am not fond of kitchens. Not even of kitchens that are easy to be fond of. Usually, humans are hostile towards things and objects they don't understand. Like the 'early man' apes in Kubrick's *2001: A Space Odyssey,* confused, afraid and reacting badly to that ultimate modular kitchen appliance of the sleek, black, mysterious monolith. But over the years, I have come to understand—or, at least, I think I do—my fear of kitchens.

While for most people, it is the part of the house from where meals appear before they are made to reappear from the refrigerator (which may or may not be in the kitchen), for me, it is the factory space where two types of people, not necessarily belonging to the same category, work: women and/or cooks. They seem to spend inordinately long hours even in circa 2023 to produce meals that are consumed in less than half the time it takes to make them. Of course, 'somebody's got to do it'—especially when the fact that I can't cook stares back at me like an ogling abyss but, the celebration of the kitchen bears sinister overtones that I can't shake off no matter how much pleasure making food in kitchens supposedly provide those who cook regularly.

Of course, it would be haraam to slag off kitchens to someone who takes genuine pleasure in spending time cooking. This pleasure, sprinkled generously with pride, is not too dissimilar than the one someone may take in wearing the hijab or smoking cigarettes, acts that are seen in the non-practitioner's eyes as subtly enforced and manufactured-to-be-made pleasurable by mass media and society. I do not understand this pleasure. But I do understand why I don't understand it.

I have grown up in an extended family of overwhelmingly, in all its senses, women, where even when my grandfather was alive till the end of Durga Pujo in 1980, my grandmother was sultan. (In 1983—it was certainly after India had won the Prudential World Cup—she and I came home after watching Kamal Amrohi's Hema Malini-starring *Razia Sultan* and she reminded me how the only female ruler of the Delhi Sultanate refused to call herself 'Sultana' as that meant 'sultan's wife (or mistress)' rather than female ruler. Home was made in the image of home she made it be, whether it be the choice of thick curtains, the choice of plants and the brass pots in which the clay ones stood, the frequency of spring cleaning (spring came twice), the Meals that rotated from mutton curry (with plenty of potatoes) and egg noodles to mutton cutlets, and luchi-aloo'r dum, with the furious whirl of a fairground merry-go-round that had broken out of its fixed carousel.

And yet, there was the kitchen.

It was moderately sized, moderately neat, although the amount of mustard oil used in our food left a black tar-like film on the wall above the stove and on the single bulb that hung from the middle of the ceiling turning it ominously into a sarson ki light. There were, in various points in my life, at least three people womanning this red walled space: my grandmother, my mother, and for a while a cook with such thick glasses that I found him strange. There was a help who stayed with us—and with whom I would go to the winter circus and jatra nights, three nights of pop theatre extravaganza that I would soon enough recognise in Ramanand Sagar's 1987 TV mega jatra, Ramayan—who, despite his thinness but because of his manness—would also help out in crushing, mixing, grinding, etc., in the kitchen.

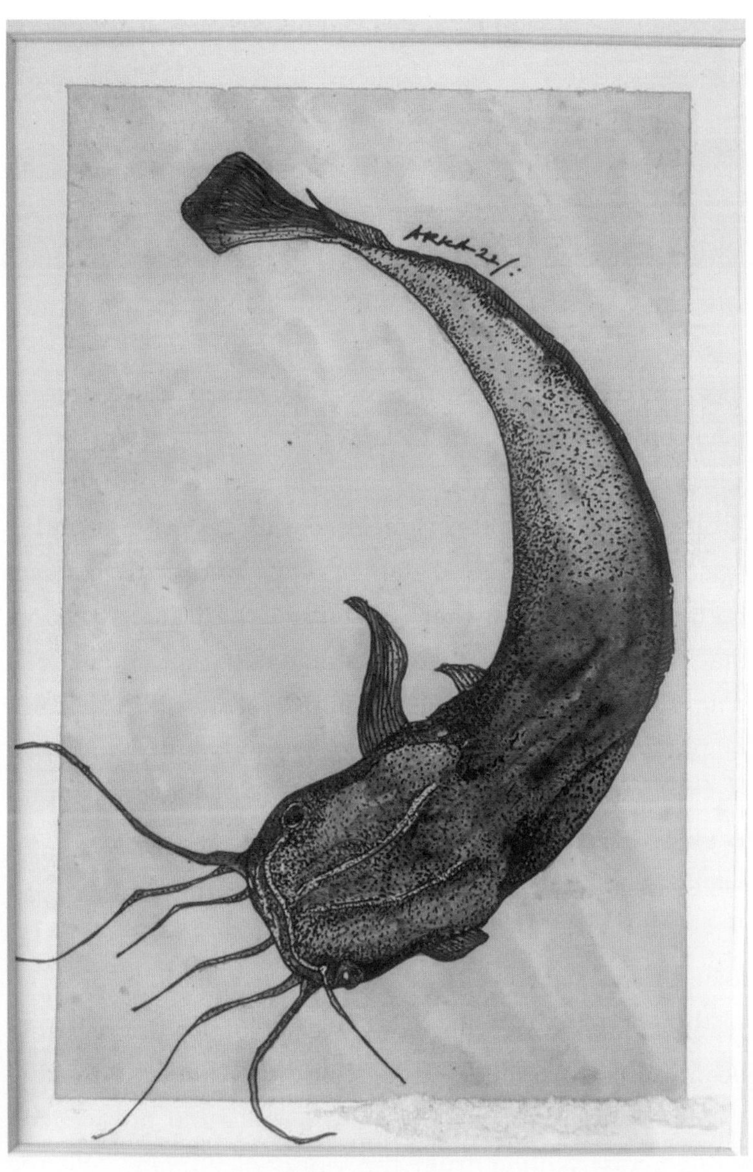

Look Back in Magur: *Untitled, 2022, Arka Das*

I reckon that this was the second-most active room I had seen in my life. The first being my maternal grandmother's kitchen. This was far more cavernous, a veritable Gollum's cave at the foot of the Misty Mountains. My maternal grandmother was more gentle, quiet, passive, literally and figuratively saun-papri soft. But inside this barebrick kitchen where a coal stove, more Hephaestus's forge than Hawkins kitchen range, lay, my Daadi sat hours on end, preparing to cook, cooking, preparing to cook, cooking...like a cross between a chef and a meth lab cook.

Let it be told that both Amma and Daadi made superb, Proustian time-recapturing meals, day in, day out, a veritable feast for each lunch and dinner. They were truly magical both in taste and in their existence—the former's magur machher jhol (more catfish soup than curry) and the latter's chingri machher malai curry (more a lake of sweetish fire of prawns than the non-existent coconut milk (malai) in her version)—were signature dishes that I have not found anywhere outside the two families. And yet, and yet, them kitchens.

***

I know, I know. Civilisations are all about appreciating beautiful and wonderful things, not just about the making and savouring of them. This is where natural phenomena fundamentally differ from the works of humans. We see a glorious view or a beautiful creature and we describe it, appreciate it, celebrate it. For those not fortunate enough to share the experience—say, the cliffhanger 1958 European Cup final that Real Madrid won over AC Milan, which also saw a duel being played out by one of football's greats Alfredo Di Stéfano and Milan's Juan 'Pepe' Schiaffino—reading about it, not just the game being described, but also about its greatness, provides second-hand pleasure from the right hands. Drinking in the beauty of a Gaitonde painting at the National Gallery of Modern Art in Delhi is a stunning experience. But reading or listening to its appreciation, being given reasons why it is so moving—'the colour [yellow] becomes the subject of the painting itself'—also holds a moving power.

Works of art or music are creations about which secondary material can become works of art themselves. Many great works of art are themselves 'secondary material' about natural phenomena, be it the beauty of a woman ('Chul tar kobekar andhokar bidishar nisha'/Her hair was the long ago dark of Vidisha's blackness, 'Bonolota Sen', Jibananda Das), the horror of depression ('More pangs will, schooled at forepangs, wilder wring,' 'No Worst, There is None,' Gerard Manley Hopkins), or the happiness that comes with the coming of a new day ('Here Comes the Sun,' George Harrison/The Beatles).

And many are in appreciation of other manmade things. The minor form taken for praising works of human creation are not to be scoffed at. I have, many a time, enjoyed a book review or an essay on music immensely without having encountered the book or music in question ever myself.

Food, in the form of the result of cooking, has brought me many times to a similar point of intersection of thing and thing being described. Except imagine someone who enjoys reading Baudelaire on Poe:

> ...Poe was a singularly solitary brain [in America]. He believed only in the immutable, in the eternal, in the self-same , and he enjoyed—a cruel privilege in a society in love with itself!—that great Machiavellian good sense which walks before the wise, like a column of light, across the desert of history.

over reading Edgar Allan Poe.

I am not unfond of food (I find fondue providing the clue for the Swiss love and talent in the plastic arts), but not overtly fond either, and certainly not celebratory about either the art of cooking or the act of eating, the latter being made to be some sort of art itself these days. The fact that there was someone I knew who was noted, with alloyed wonder as well as a social curio, for knowing *what* cheese to have with *what* wine, reaffirmed my belief in appreciation being able to turn into a vestigial act, a foppery.

Like all things worth valuing—and a society should, indeed, be judged by its ability to value its things—whether it be power tools or furniture, I understand the need to celebrate fine cooking. Just because I don't get opera or <Mad Men> doesn't mean they're rubbish. The same way I would not expect my writings on the beauty to be found in some snot sculpture to be dismissed along with an unappreciated art form. But cultural appreciation—whether of conceptual art of the kind by Maurizio Cattelan's 2019 *Comedian*, a banana stuck to the gallery wall by duct tape, or Rabindrasangeet—is essentially determined by how it is propped up, infused with 'artness'.

In the case of food, such infusion has a particular advantage. Everyone may not listen to ghazals, or care for Mughal miniatures, but everyone eats, and being adventurous about eating is what being adventurous about setting off on adventures once held: broadening one's horizons while finding pleasure, and getting street cred while at it. The gourmand and the gourmet are today's nobility and patrons of fine art. The problem with everyone seeking to become a Wajid Ali Shah in the age of information and opinion overload, however, is that it gives you the illusion of objectivity, one thing that things deemed 'art' or 'fine things' are devoid of.

I have tried hard in my formative and post-formative years to develop a taste for jazz. I have failed, but not miserably. Unlike the case of the boy who points out that the emperor is actually not wearing any clothes, my inability to like jazz is neither because jazz is crap (Philip Larkin can't be wrong) nor because I have a jazz gene missing. I am simply deaf to it, like so many people are, to say, punk rock without feeling miserable about being denied its pleasure. Singing hosannas to cooking and meals holds no value for me and give me no pleasure. Also, I have noticed that there is a good chance that I literally have 'bad taste' when it comes to eating.

My grandmother's magur machher jhol is so supremely tasty, and yet it is not on any single restaurant or hole-in-the-wall applauded by so-and-so's menu. The same holds for 'delicacies' like canned baked beans, my other grandmother's spicy fried potatoes (diced, but with their skin intact) kachori-saabzi from Mohan Bhandar off Chowringhee in Kolkata, chilli chicken (with bone, and bone-dry peppered with green chillies) from Chung Wah, again near Chowringhee, and even the 'despised' Chauteaubriand ('It's become ghastly!') from Mocambo on Park Street...

It seems that in the matter of taste, I don't have good taste. So along with the formative fear and hostility towards kitchens, the other reason for me not taking to these cooking rooms like pork to a pot is because their functional appeal—even as an eater, since I can't cook—is lost on me. The thought of cooking a meal (and I have tried a few times), even 'for pleasure,' gives me the heebie-jeebies.

I have burned a whole pan of prawns after a phone call went on for too long. I have bought a wholesome can of chili con carne, which upon seeing a stove at my disposal, poured its contents into a pan smeared with olive oil and thereby destroyed the pre-cooked meal. I have stuck to instant soup, toast, canned tuna and sardines, and microwaved rice—it's a delicate two-step process—when absolutely necessary. I have made it my mission to always be able to afford cooked meals so as to not make the aforementioned 'absolutely necessary' circumstances arise. And yes, I do bear the palpable guilt of being an anachronism of someone who never learnt to cook, and never will since the idea itself is incredibly tiresome for me.

The simmering, the stirring, the mixing, the mixie-ing, the portioning, the apportioning, the adding, the watching, the pinch-ing, the table-spooning, the cooling, the rising, the chopping, the dicing, the straining...An onlooker would very well describe me looking into a kitchen: 'He cried in a whisper at some image, at some vision—he cried out twice, a cry that was no more than a breath: "The horror! The horror!"'

The kitchen, for me, is the site of crimes that are not criminalised. No matter how many devastatingly attractive rasois I see in the movies—with kitchen islands around which family members gather perfunctorily as if it's the balcony, with gleaming copper pans hanging from hooks like some post-impressionistic still-life—I recoil from them, these deceptively bright, satanic mills around which cultures and civilisations are made to hang like aprons and pans.

I gaze into the kitchen and the kitchen gazes back at me. 'Hypocrite eater, my semblance, my brother!' it tells me as I shut the door on its face each and every time.

TWO GRANDMUMS, TWO RECIPES

MAGUR MACHHER JHOL (AMMA STYLE)

Ingredients:

1. Maagur maach (Catfish)
2. Medium-sized potatoes
3. Brinjal
4. Green chillies
5. Zeera (Cumin)
6. Turmeric
7. Salt

Preparation:

1. Dice potatoes lengthwise for the gravy, coat them in salt and turmeric.
2. Dice a brinjal into long pieces, coat them in salt and turmeric.
3. Clean the fish pieces, coat them in salt and turmeric.
4. Grind the cumin or make a coarse paste of cumin.

Cooking:

1. Heat a kadai and add mustard oil.
2. Once the oil is hot, take the fish pieces, fry them in oil and keep aside.
3. Next, fry the brinjal lightly and keep them aside.
4. Add the potatoes, fry them lightly in oil.
5. Next, add turmeric, chillies, and salt.

6. Add water according to the amount of gravy you want, cover, and let it cook.
7. Once the potatoes are almost boiled, add the fried fish.
8. Add the cumin paste.
9. Call the grandson for a taste check and switch off flame.

CHINGRI MACHHER MALAIKARI (DAADI STYLE)

Ingredients:

1. Medium-sized prawns
2. Medium-sized potatoes
3. Red onions
4. Garlic
5. Green chillies
6. Salt
7. Sugar
8. Turmeric

Preparation:

1. Clean prawns, dry them and coat them with turmeric.
2. Cube two medium-sized potatoes and coat them with turmeric.
3. Coarsely chop the red onions.
4. Paste the onions.
5. Paste the garlic.
6. Paste the green chillies.

Cooking:

1. Heat a kadai and add mustard oil.
2. Once the oil is hot, take the prawns first and fry them lightly and keep aside.
3. Next, fry the potatoes and keep them aside.
4. Add sugar to the oil, lower the flame and let the sugar turn a rich brown, but do not let it burn.
5. Once caramelised, add the garlic paste, coarsely chopped onions, chilli paste, add a pinch of red chilli powder. Fry till the ingredients come together.
6. Add turmeric, onion paste, more garlic paste, salt, and fry well.
7. Add the lightly fried potatoes and the prawns.
8. Add as much water as you would like for the gravy, cover and bring it to boil.
9. Add sugar.
10. Call the grandson for a taste check and switch off flame.

ACKNOWLEDGEMENTS

Sticking to facts can be an onerous task. It requires a certain kind of imaginative spirit that tells the mind, 'Listen, I've got some good news, and some bad news. The bad news first: We have to deal with real things. But the good news is, the belief that refrigerators can talk in a subsonic, electrical hum language is a fact about such a belief. So...'

My superb editor Arpita Das kept reminding me about this 'good news-bad news' business, especially daunting for someone who had not really ventured out beyond a Lakshmanrekha in the realm of non-fiction. Her belief in the ordered chaos my essays could take, without falling into the porcelain monorail of 'beautiful narrative non-fiction' gave much courage, including a couple of rounds of the Dutch variety. I thank her from the bottom of my ink well.

My day job at *The Economic Times* gave me what writing residencies provide proper writers—the stability of a sturdy table. My work in *ET* provides me access to an ideas and words gym that gave me the muscles to deal with the 'longer, stranger stuff' here.

One of the essays in this book, 'I Singe the Body Electric,' in its shorter form came out in *Open* magazine in 2013 that the-then editor Manu Joseph had commissioned me to write. The story that lies inside 'Roti Rising' was written as a draft for a short comic book story for the magazine *Comixense*. Its editor Orijit Sen had another story in mind, so I chased that leaving this story more or less in its current form tucked inside the 'essay'.

The rest of the writing in this book is spanking new.

Along with the rest of the images in this book, there is one original artwork—a colour drawing by the wonderful artist (and fab drummer of the band Easy Rider) Arka Das. His picture of the 'magur machh' holds a central place in our living room.

My parents have been the constant demand side to my idiosyncratic supply side. Trying to explain to my father what I will be writing in my weekly Bengali column in *Ei Samay* each week provides me clarity and exasperation in one heady cocktail. Banter mixed with information has been the bread and batter they have served me, and each other, for years. It remains a default diet for me.

'The dog ate my homework' was an option I had planned to use if I managed to leave this book unfinished. Laili, our brown-eyed girl who is equal parts fascinated by supine cats under parked cars as well as by laptops that never seem to shut their mouths, never gave me that opportunity (read: excuse). This is my first book under her thrall. May she like the smell of its pages.

And without Oyndrila, nothing would have been possible. She has been my sparring partner, demonic disciplinarian, scholar on tap, IT girl, drinking buddy, and carver-out of spacetime. If anyone is on this side of the page and world with me, it is her.